# How to Design and Post Information on a Corporate Intranet

## Dedication

This book is dedicated to Sue, Rachel and Lewis.

One day they may read it and come to understand what I do when I put my suit on.

# How to Design and Post Information on a Corporate Intranet

## Bryan Hopkins

Gower

Croft Road
Aldershot
Hampshire  GU11 3HR

Gower
Old Post Road
Brookfield
Vermont  05036
USA

**British Library Cataloguing in Publication Data**

Hopkins, Bryan
How to design and post information on a corporate intranet
1. Local are networks (computer networks)
I. Title
004.6'8


ISBN  0 566 07981 X

**Library of Congress Cataloging-In-Publication Data**

Hopkins, Bryan, 1954–
    How to design and post information on a corporate intranet / Bryan Hopkins.
        p.    cm.
    Includes bibliographical references.
    ISBN 0–566–07981–X (wire bound)
    1. Intranets (computer networks)   2. Web sites  Design  Planning
    I. Title.
    HD30.385.H66  1997
    651.7'9  dcdc21                                                 97–28408
                                                                        CIP

Typeset in Microsoft® Office for Windows™ by Paul Newcombe of Sheffield and printed in Great Britain
by Hartnolls of Bodmin.

# Contents

# List of illustrations

# Preface

We live in a world that is steadily becoming more and more dominated by information. Fortunes are made and lost each day by people acquiring information before others do. We are slowly becoming info-junkies, desperate to get the next fix even if we don't know what it is or if it is going to do us any good at all.

The rise of the corporate intranet is yet another twist in the spiral, and a major twist at that. The intranet provides us with, in theory at least, access to everything that our organisation knows. The effective and efficient use of intranet technology could well lead us on to the age of the learning organisation. However, it can only do this if we make it do this. And to that end we need to think seriously about what information we post on an intranet and how that should be presented.

Although the Internet, intranets and web design are new technologies, much has already been written about them, in itself a symptom of our information society. Most of this is aimed at technically competent people who can find their way around an HTML or Java program. It does not address itself to the growing number of people working in training and personnel whose daily task it is to present information. What I therefore want to do in this book is to show non-programmers how to go about designing and posting information on an internal web, using software tools that do all the complex programming for you. If, after reading it, you want to find out more about HTML or Java, you can find many books on these subjects.

I am not now a programmer myself, although I did start out in the field of training design as a programmer. My work nowadays as a training consultant is to look at performance problems within organisations and propose ways of dealing with them, which often involve providing staff with better information and training. I therefore make no apologies for looking in this book at both providing information and designing some simple computer-based training. I think that too often these areas are seen as separate, and that organisations expect different departments to look after them. One thing the intranet will do is to blur the distinctions between the two.

Improving performance means looking at what people do and finding ways of helping them to do it better. Providing information is an important way of doing this, and my experience tells me that people will only use information if it does help them to do something better, quicker or more easily. The methods I outline in this book come from my realisation that the best people to decide how information should be presented are the users themselves. Therefore, this book places a lot of emphasis on presenting information from the point of view of: 'What will the user do with this information?'. Will they complete a form quicker and more accurately? Will they manage colleagues more effectively? Will they know what to do to live up to their organisation's values?

It is surprising how easy it is for those of us charged with the responsibility for writing something to feel that we must appear to be the experts. We therefore think we must be able to work out all the content by ourselves or with the help of a few books. This ivory tower approach can then often lead to us spending hours agonising over what needs to go into a document, when a few well-placed phone calls or an hour with potential users of the information could solve our problems very quickly. Throughout this book, therefore, I suggest that you involve users at all stages in the design process.

Looking at information from a performance point of view helps us to convert it from something passive, that sits there, does nothing and may often be ignored, into something active, that people seek out and use.

The approach I describe in this book comes from the way in which I would tackle a design project where I start out with nothing but a general description of the problem. You may not be in this position, so some parts of the process may not be relevant to you. This is why I describe this book as a toolkit: you take out what you need. But even if you feel that your responsibility is simply to design pages, I would urge you to read the other parts of the book. These introduce skills that can help you to do this part of your job with more confidence and imagination.

I wish you well.

Bryan Hopkins

# Acknowledgements

I must offer my thanks to:

- colleagues at ACT Consultants, whose support over the years has helped me put together the ideas within this book

- the following people who provided me with help and information, read through manuscripts and put me straight on different issues:

  Neil Hughes, Department for Education and Employment, Sheffield
  Norman Lamont, Scottish Widows Fund and Life Assurance Society, Edinburgh
  Mark Stimson, Aimtech Europe, London

- Paul Newcombe, who designed the layout for the book

# Introduction
## What is this book about?

# Introduction
## What is this book about?

*'It was a bright cold day in April, and the clocks were striking thirteen.'*

This is the first line of George Orwell's *1984*, a line that intrigues the reader by its blend of familiarity and difference. It is a line that makes you want to carry on and find out more about this place that is just like what we know yet is not quite the same. *1984* was a very successful book, but there was more to it than the first line. As with any best-seller, each page has a quality that makes you want to carry on, to read just the next page before putting the light out at bedtime.

That is not only true about novels: it applies to successful factual information as well. Whenever we present someone with information, we need to present it in such a way that the reader wants to look at the next stage. So often we find dull, flabby information that sits there on the page or on screen and that makes no effort to engage us. Such information is a waste of everything that has gone into its creation: of the trees that were felled to make the paper, of the reader's time in wading through it and the writer's time in putting it together.

The most important people to consider when we are presenting information are the readers. They are the ones who decide whether it is of value or not. If they like it and find it useful, they will use it. If they do not find it useful, they will not use it. This becomes particularly important as we move to electronic means of spreading information, as it is inherently harder to read information off a screen. Our eyes find it more tiring, and we do not have the same control over the screen as we do over the pages of a book.

Also, when the reader knows that 'what I want is in there somewhere if only I could find it', they start to become frustrated. So-called 'information anxiety' is a modern affliction, caused by thinking that what you need is available somewhere. We therefore need to make sure that information is easy to find.

# Who is it written for?

This book is aimed at those people with responsibility for designing content for their organisational intranet. Such materials can cover a broad spectrum, from passive information such as policy statements through to interactive training materials, incorporating multimedia elements. The intranet concept is starting to blur the distinction between information and training, and I think that it is important for anyone involved in presenting information on their intranet to have an understanding of the different skills required at each end of the spectrum.

The sorts of people who will find this book of value will be:

- Training or human resource managers, who may be interested in some new approaches to training delivery and design

- Training designers, for whom on-line training delivery may be new

- Corporate communications teams, who are moving from paper-based delivery media to electronic, in which they may have no experience

- Information technology managers, who know the differences between protocols but need to know more about what they can enable

- Departmental managers, who, charged with implementing new policies using the intranet as a medium, want to know how to package the information

- Anyone who is taking on the role of managing an intranet site for an office or department, the 'webmasters'

 # How should you use the book?

I have written this book from the viewpoint of a project manager. I have assumed that you as the reader will want to pick up and use some of these skills immediately, so I have laid out the content systematically, starting at the beginning and finishing at the end of the process.

Depending on the nature of your work, you may not want to read everything. Those of you who want to know how to present a simple policy statement may only need certain chapters, while those of you developing an intranet-based training programme will probably want to work all the way through the book. Use it like a toolbox: look in it and pull out what you find useful.

There are a number of case studies that run through the book. These serve to illustrate how to apply the process in a real-life situation.

**Chapter 1** looks at the technical side of the intranet in simple terms. It describes the main features of the most important part of the intranet, the browser. If you understand this you will be able to start to use it effectively.

**Chapter 2** examines why writing for the screen and for paper are different. If you are used to paper-based delivery you should read this so that you can start to appreciate some of the factors that will constrain or open up your writing. You may also need to pass some of this information on to internal customers who do not realise that there are significant differences.

**Chapter 3** considers project management issues. If there are likely to be a number of different elements to your design and development project, or if you think you need some help in this area, have a look at this chapter.

**Chapter 4** describes how to go about drawing a profile of your target groups, the people who will be using your information. Always keep your likely reader in mind as you write.

**Chapter 5** is the heart of the book, and looks at some different techniques for breaking down, or 'chunking', your information. The emphasis is very much on working with the end users to develop information that they find useful.

**Chapter 6** covers the art of clear, effective writing. Poorly written English destroys the clarity of information, so this chapter offers you a set of guidelines on how to keep your text as easy to understand as possible.

**Chapter 7** looks at screen design. It offers basic information on the use of colour and graphics and the importance of providing adequate navigational aids for the user. It also looks at how to use such features as tables and frames. This chapter shows how you can use Microsoft FrontPage to design your pages but you can apply the principles discussed to whichever method you use for adding the HTML code.

**Chapter 8** moves us on from how to deliver information to providing interactivity through the use of specialised software packages such as Jamba and IconAuthor. These employ different technologies that allow a designer to develop interactive training materials.

**Chapter 9** describes how to build quality in to your site. This includes how to make sure that your site is useful, has style and has no programming errors.

**Chapter 10** examines the issues of implementation and what you can do to make sure that you keep receiving feedback on the quality of your information.

# Chapter

# What is an intranet?

# How does an intranet work?

There are many different ways in which computers can be connected together in a network. In order for each of the computers to be able to send data back and forth, they must all speak the same language, or *protocol*. The protocol that the Internet and intranets use is called the Transmission Control Protocol/Internet Protocol, usually just called TCP/IP.

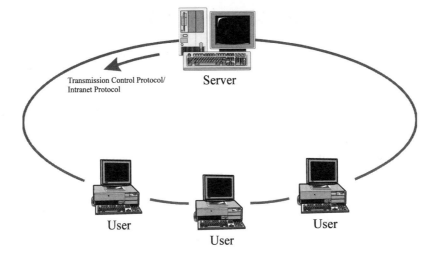

*Figure 1.1: A simple TCP/IP network*

Anyone wanting to use an intranet uses a piece of software called a 'browser'. There are many different browsers on the market, but the most common ones are Netscape Navigator and Internet Explorer. However, they all work in a similar way and look very much alike. Figure 1.2 shows what Netscape Navigator v.3 looks like:

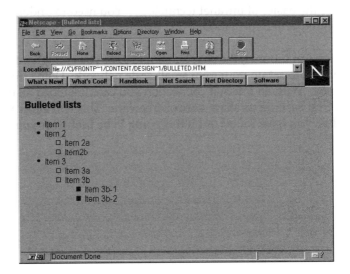

*Figure 1.2: Netscape Navigator v.3*

This is Internet Explorer v.3:

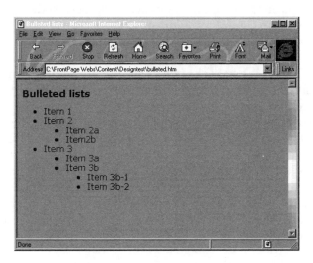

*Figure 1.3: Microsoft Internet Explorer v.3*

What happens when you load a browser? It first checks to see if your computer has a TCP/IP connection. If it does, it will then start to look for another computer in the network. It will be told which one to look for by a setting within the browser. This computer is the one identified in the box called 'Location', 'URL' or 'Address' (depending on which browser you are using). If you are familiar with connecting to the Internet, you will know that Netscape, for example, first looks for a computer called 'http://home.netscape.com/'. A browser set up to use an intranet will probably look for the computer that stores the main pages for the organisation's intranet. This name is part of what is called the URL, or Universal Resource Locator. This is effectively the computer's address, in the same way as every house in a town has an address.

URLs can seem very complicated. Let's pull 'http://home.netscape.com/' apart and see what each part means.

*http* stands for Hypertext Transfer Protocol and tells the browser that it is going to look for a file written using a special programming language called Hypertext Mark-up Language, usually referred to as HTML. When it knows how the file has been written it can read it and make sense of it when it receives it. By convention this is followed by a colon and two forward slashes (://).

*home.netscape* is the name of the computer where the particular file is stored. More properly, it is known as the **domain name**.

*com* is a code that the Internet uses to identify a computer as being part of a commercial organisation (other codes are, for example, *gov* for government bodies and *ac* for educational establishments).

After the com is a forward slash. This may be followed by a series of names, or perhaps just one, often *index.htm*. This is the name of the file stored on this server that the browser wants to read. The .htm extension (sometimes also written as .html) identifies it as a file written in HTML. By convention, the first page on any web server should be called 'index.htm', and browsers will automatically load this file if no other file name is given.

The computer that the browser is looking for must be running special web server software. This acts like a storekeeper. The request for the file comes in from the network and the web server runs off, reads the file and sends a copy of what it contains back to the computer which asked for it.

The browser receives the data and, because it knows that it has been coded in HTML, translates it on to the screen as text, graphics, audio or video.

That is essentially how an intranet works. The key element is the HTML programming of the files stored on the server. HTML is what is known as an *interpreted* programming language, like Basic. This means that when a programmer writes the code, it is left as it is written and is not converted into a different format for the computer to read (which is what happens with *compiled* languages, such as C++). When the computer is told to execute the program, it reads the file and interprets what to do. This has a crucial advantage as far as an intranet is concerned. It means that if a PC reads it, the PC software can decide what the PC needs to do in response. If a UNIX workstation reads it, the UNIX software works out how the UNIX computer must respond. And so on, for other computer types such as Apple Macs, and even, in theory and soon in practice, such diverse pieces of equipment as mobile phones and dishwashers. Therefore our HTML file should, in theory, display in exactly the same way on any type of computer on the network.

HTML is a relatively young language, but it has a set of commands that is quickly becoming more and more powerful. These may be to display the next piece of text in a different size of typeface or colour, or insert a graphic file. It may inform the browser that the following piece of text is linked to another file on the server or elsewhere, and that if the user clicks their mouse on this text, the browser must find that file. This is the most important feature about HTML, because this is what allows *hyperlinking*. This is where the user can select information from normal passages of text, rather than from formal tables of contents, indexes or directory listings of files with unhelpful names.

Hyperlinking is a computer technique that allows the same process as happens when you are looking for an explanation of something in a dictionary or encyclopaedia. For example, if you look up the word 'concept' in the *Hutchinson Dictionary of Ideas*, you find:

**'... in philosophy the term concept has replaced the more ambiguous "⇨ idea" '**

So you can look up 'idea':

**'... a term that has had a variety of technical usages an ⇨ innate idea is ...'**

So you can look up 'innate', and so on. Some theories say that this is a more effective way of delivering information because this interlinking of ideas mimics the way our brains work.

Back in the early days of HTML programming, say all of two years ago, if you wanted to put up pages on the Internet or an intranet you had to learn how to program in HTML. Although it is not a particularly difficult language to learn, it did mean that it became the province of the 'techies', who were not necessarily the best communicators! Fortunately, software technology has now moved on so that you can use packages resembling ordinary word processors, such as NetObjects Fusion or FrontPage, that generate the HTML code for you. This is making intranet development much more accessible to those of us with neither the time nor the inclination to learn HTML programming.

# What are the main features of a browser?

If you are going to design information that a user can access easily through a browser, you must know what a browser looks like to the user and what features it has. Although there are many different browsers in use, they are all somewhat similar and there are many features common to all. Also, if you are familiar with the Windows interface you will be able to identify the usual Windows functionality.

Take a look at the browser screen below. This shows you the main features you need to know:

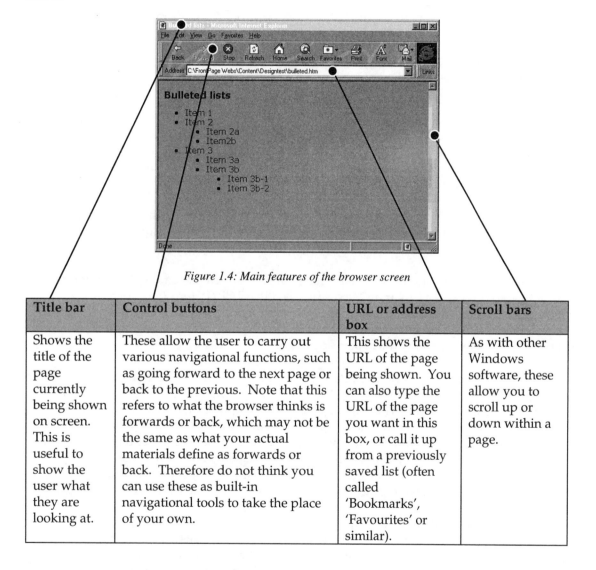

*Figure 1.4: Main features of the browser screen*

| Title bar | Control buttons | URL or address box | Scroll bars |
|---|---|---|---|
| Shows the title of the page currently being shown on screen. This is useful to show the user what they are looking at. | These allow the user to carry out various navigational functions, such as going forward to the next page or back to the previous. Note that this refers to what the browser thinks is forwards or back, which may not be the same as what your actual materials define as forwards or back. Therefore do not think you can use these as built-in navigational tools to take the place of your own. | This shows the URL of the page being shown. You can also type the URL of the page you want in this box, or call it up from a previously saved list (often called 'Bookmarks', 'Favourites' or similar). | As with other Windows software, these allow you to scroll up or down within a page. |

If you are not comfortable with using a browser, make sure that you get the chance to spend some time using one, to move around your own intranet or the Internet itself. It is only by doing this that you will start to develop an understanding of how best to use the software's abilities, and hence to design useful materials for your intranet's users.

# How can I set up an intranet?

If by now you are itching to get going but are frustrated because you do not have an intranet to play with, stay calm. Setting one up is very easy. You can even do it at home if you have two computers with a network connection. This section will explain briefly how to go about it. If you do need more detail, there are a number of excellent technically oriented books available that can help.

Try Chapter 3 of Ryan Bernard's *The Corporate Intranet*, published by Wiley, ISBN 0-471-14929-2.

## Set up a TCP/IP network

The starting point for an intranet is a network with computers running the TCP/IP protocol. There are a large number of different protocols in use, and not all networks use TCP/IP. If your network has a number of UNIX servers, such as Sun, Silicon Graphics or RS/6000 computers, your network may already have this connection. Similarly, you are in luck if you have a network of PCs running Windows 95 or Windows NT. However, if you are running Windows 3.11, you will not have a TCP/IP connection. If you are not sure whether you do have one, explore the network settings on your computers and look for anything referring to TCP/IP. If you do this and find reference to an 'IP address', which will be a four-digit number such as 148.45.78.14, you are indeed running TCP/IP.

The most likely case where you will not be running the protocol is on Windows 3.11 systems. In that case, you can obtain a disk from Microsoft called the 'TCP/IP for Windows for Workgroups'. You can download this from the Microsoft World Wide Web pages at ftp.microsoft.com\bussys\msclient\wfw. Follow the instructions for installing it on the machines in your network and you will be ready to go.

This will introduce you to the world of TCP/IP addresses. On a TCP/IP network, every computer must have a four-digit number as its name, similar to that mentioned above. If your network is purely internal and there are no other TCP/IP computers attached to it anywhere, you can choose any numbers you want (as long as the numbers are each 255 or less). However, you must not give a number at random to a computer that is a server on the Internet, as every computer on the Internet must have a unique number. If by chance you duplicated an IP address that already exists, you could cause chaos! Follow the instructions that come with your protocol package to set these addresses and make various other settings.

Wait a minute. I said earlier that the computer name is something like home.netscape.com. Where does the four-digit number fit in? The IP address is what the network recognises, but because we as users find such numbers hard to remember, part of the TCP/IP protocol software on each computer keeps a list of IP addresses and their associated names. Therefore, when we tell the browser to look for home.netscape.com, it checks the list to see what the IP address of that computer is, and off it goes.

On your intranet you can make up your own domain names that are relevant to the computer. For example, you could identify the computers as:

- bryan.mycompany.com
- sophie.mycompany.com
- webserver1.mycompany.com
- and so on

## Set up a web server

Next, you will need some web server software. Web server software is designed to receive requests from the network for intranet and Internet materials and send the required data back. There are a large number of web server packages available for the different operating systems, such as Microsoft's Internet Information Server, Quarterdeck's WebSTAR and Netscape's FastTrack or Enterprise Servers. Each is designed for particular operating systems and for particular levels of usage.

> To get started, try the Internet for simple servers at:
>
> - **http://www.city.net/win-httpd/ for Windows 3.11**
>
> - **http://website.ora.com/checkitout/demo.html for Windows 95**

Web servers are often very simple beasts. Generally you simply load them then ignore them. They may not even have any facilities for adjustment, although servers designed for heavy usage will have sophisticated features built in to them that you will need to explore.

### 3. Make an HTML test file

The traditional way of testing out your skills in a new programming language is to create a file that displays 'Hello world' on the screen.

There are various ways of doing that for your first intranet page:

**1. Use a text editor with HTML**

It is beyond the scope of this book to explain how to program HTML. However, you should find that if you type the code below, exactly as it is, into a simple text editor, such as Notepad or Wordpad, then save it under the filename HELLO.HTM, it will display "Hello world" on your browser.

```
<HTML><HEAD>
<TITLE>Hello world test page</TITLE>
</HEAD><BODY><P>Hello world
</BODY></HTML>
```

There are a large number of books available that will show you how to code in HTML.

**2. Download free HTML software**

If you are using Microsoft Word 6, you can download an upgrade to it called Internet Assistant from the Microsoft World Wide Web pages. You should be able to find this at http://www.microsoft.com/word/Internet/ia/default.htm. When you have installed it, you will find that after typing in your text and choosing Save or Save as, you can select HTML from the list of file types. When you have done this, the toolbar buttons change to those appropriate for HTML editing. It is in reality a fairly simple piece of software, and you may not find it very useful once you start to experiment more seriously.

Alternatively, there is a freeware program called GNN Press that you can download from http://www.tools.gnn.com/. This is a simple WYSIWYG (what you see is what you get) HTML editor that will certainly help you to get started on creating a web.

### 3. Buy some serious HTML editing software

There are more and more heavy-duty HTML editors appearing on the market now. They differ in how they work and to what extent they shield you from HTML coding, so it would pay to ask around before investing in them. Some of the packages you will find are:

| | |
|---|---|
| **Microsoft FrontPage for Windows 95** | • True WYSIWYG interface<br><br>• Does not allow any HTML editing at all in v1.1, but does in FrontPage 97<br><br>• Front Page Explorer displays linkages between web pages |
| **NetObjects Fusion** | • True WYSIWYG interface<br><br>• Very intuitive to use |
| **HoTMeTaL Pro** | • WYSI nearly WYG<br><br>• Available for Windows 3.11<br><br>• Needs some HTML knowledge |
| **Asymetrix WebPublisher** | • Easy to use<br><br>• Limited look to pages<br><br>• Available for Windows 3.11 |

Any of these packages will get you started, but with varying degrees of ease.

Once you have created your test file you will need to use a browser to see it.

## 4 Open a browser

As mentioned above, there are a number of browsers available, but the two market leaders are Netscape Navigator and Microsoft Internet Explorer. They are similar to look at and use, although they have some different features that become significant as you start to look at more sophisticated web pages. To start off with download both from the Netscape and Microsoft World Wide Web sites and try them out.

When you have installed the browser and loaded it, type the URL of your test file into the address box, press Return, and, if everything is in place, your 'Hello world' message should appear.

If it does not, the most likely problems are that the two computers are not exchanging TCP/IP messages or that the server software is not recognising the TCP/IP protocol package you have installed. Whatever happens, use the diagnostic tools built into the protocol packages (such as Ping) to try to find out what is happening. If that does not help, you may need to look for technical help.

That, as briefly as is possible, is how you can go about setting up a small intranet. Once you have done so, you can then start designing your information.

# What is so important about intranets anyway?

To finish this chapter, it may be of value to you to understand why so much interest is being shown in intranets within organisations.

Because intranets have only been around for about two years it is still difficult to say what their implications might be for an organisation. After all, it took 40 years to work out how to make anything useful out of the electric motor. There are already some examples of how companies have taken intranet technology and have used it to improve the way parts of their business work.

- **Silicon Graphics** used an intranet to eliminate the need to fill in paper forms for stationery orders.

- **Booz Allen & Hamilton**, a US-based consultancy firm, used an intranet to develop a 'knowledge base' which allowed their consultants to consolidate their individual experiences into a resource available to all.

- **Chevron Oil** has an intranet that provides information on the history and structure of the company, its technical services, its customers and its employees, among other things.

Why have they found their intranets so valuable? In the first instance, using an intranet to deliver information means that everyone in the organisation has instant access to up-to-date information. Paper-based information ages rapidly: in a large organisation telephone directories are probably out of date before they have been printed, whereas an on-line directory can be updated immediately there is a change.

But intranet technology offers more than just up-to-date information. Why these companies and rapidly increasing numbers of others are showing such a keen interest is that the technology driving the Internet and intranets offers a way completely to redefine the ways in which computers are used within organisations. At the time of writing we use specialised software dedicated to specific tasks, such as word processors to write and databases to store information. We use e-mail to communicate and computer-based training programs to learn. It is rare to find instances where these are integrated into a single application. Browser technology allows just that.

Organisational information can be stored in central databases and browsers can pull it off when it is needed in a format that is relevant to what the user needs. As a simple example, a user can open the browser to run a training program that accesses stored information and their success in the training can automatically be logged back on the database. During the course of the training they may wish to send an e-mail to someone about the subject. If they find there are subjects they need more training on, they can look at the Training Department's booking form and make arrangements to do this extra training. And all from within the browser, as they are doing it.

It is this new dimension of flexibility that is most exciting about the technology. We still do not really know what the possibilities are for intranets. There are some sources listed in the bibliography that look at this subject in more detail.

# Key points from the chapter

- Intranets are based on the same hardware and software technologies that drive the Internet, hence the similarity in name.

- You need to be familiar with how a browser works before you can start to design effective information.

- Setting up your own intranet is neither difficult nor expensive.

- Intranets have the potential to revolutionise both the way computers are used within organisations and how information is delivered to employees.

# Chapter 2

# Why are writing for paper and the screen different?

How to Design and Post Information on a Corporate Intranet

# Chapter 2
## Why are writing for paper and the screen different?

After reading this chapter you will be able to:

- describe why you have to take a different approach to writing when you are preparing materials to be read from a screen rather than from paper

- state five guidelines to follow when writing for the screen

If you have spent any time at all using a computer you will know that reading from a screen is very different to reading from a page. For that reason, when we write material that users will read from a screen we must structure and present it appropriately.

The difference in writing styles caused by the change from paper-based to intranet-based information delivery may cause difficulties. If you are asked by a senior manager to transfer exactly what he or she has written directly on to the intranet, you need to think about these issues. Otherwise, there is a real danger that the information will fall flat. This chapter will give you some arguments you can offer if you do need to convince someone that you or they need to do some substantial editing or restructuring. Chapter 3 will cover some of the broader consultancy skills that you can use to help get this message across.

# What are the differences?

First, there are the technical issues:

## Shape of the page or screen

Computer screens are in a landscape rather than a portrait format. This means that the width of text tends to be greater than the height, the reverse of what happens on paper. Why is this important? As we read a line of text we build up the meaning of the line in our short-term memories, and then temporarily store it when we get to the end of the line. Our eyes then track back to the start of the next line and we repeat the process, except that our brain has to add the content of the new line on to the stored-up information. Now, our brains can only hold about seven items in short-term memory, so the longer the line, the more words and the greater demands we are placing on it. Therefore a computer screen's landscape format can place greater demands on the reader, which will make it harder for them to follow the information.

Try this as an experiment. Which of these is easier to read?

> As we read a line of text we build up the meaning of the line in our short-term memories, and then temporarily store it when we get to the end of the line. Our eyes then track back to the start of the next line and we repeat the process, except that our brain has to add the content of the new line on to the stored-up information.

> As we read a line of text we build up the meaning of the line in our short-term memories, and then temporarily store it when we get to the end of the line. Our eyes then track back to the start of the next line and we repeat the process, except that our brain has to add the content of the new line on to the stored-up information.

You probably found the second easier to read.

The way browsers and HTML work together does not help either. The length of a line on screen is determined by the size of the browser window, and this is controlled by the user. If they want to set up a wide-screen browser, they can, and they will then have long lines to read. There are ways of coding your pages to prevent this happening. We will see how to do this in Chapter 7.

## Radiated not reflected light

When we read from paper, we are using light that has been reflected off the paper. However, when we read off a screen, we are looking at light that has been radiated by the screen. This tends to be more intense, and is harder on the eyes and hence more tiring.

Then there are the practical issues:

## Amount of information per page or screen

You can fit a lot of information on to one side of a piece of paper. That is immediately available to the user without their having to turn over or find another piece. The amount of information available on a single area of a screen is much smaller, so users will have to scroll up and down or load other pages to read the same amount of information.

Screen-based information must therefore be as concise as possible.

## Turning backwards and forwards

When we read a book to find out how to do something we often flip backwards and forwards, to see how two steps fit together, or to check out understanding of something on a previous page, for example. To do this we can look at several pages more or less at the same time, but with a computer screen this is not possible. We can then get into a muddle by flipping back and forth between different screens, trying to retain and integrate lots of information. This can happen when a user is working within an information or help system, or if they are using another application, such as a spreadsheet, for which they need some outside information.

This also applies where we have to scroll up and down within a document to find different pieces of information. Think about times when you have had to read and analyse something in a long document on a screen. Scrolling makes our eyes move in unnatural ways, and this can be tiring for them.

## Position on the user's desk

When we read a book we automatically put it where we find it most comfortable or convenient. This may be close to our eyes to make out some small print or further away if we need space in front of us. In other words, we have control over the book. However, a computer screen is usually fixed in place, and it has control over us.

## Losing our place

As we go through our working days, when we find some things that are particularly useful, we make a note of them by sticking a Post-it® to that page, or by turning a corner of the page down. This makes it easy to find again. It is not so easy with computer systems. The bookmarking systems on browsers have some value, but if you keep on saving bookmarks you quickly find that you have a list that is so long you need a bookmark to find your way to your bookmark!

## The user controls the look

If you are used to desktop publishing, you will know how the look of a document is affected by the choice of typefaces that you make. You also know that the printed documents will all look exactly the same.

This is not the case with browsers. You as the author can say that a particular line is going to be a heading, but the user chooses the size and typeface of the font. If they want to read everything in a script typeface, they can. We can assume that most people will choose something sensible and easy to read, but this is not guaranteed!

Look at these two Netscape windows displaying the same information:

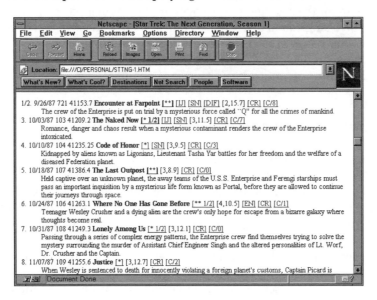

*Figure 2.1: A likely Netscape window*

This is the more likely display, a landscape format with text showing in Times Roman. But there is nothing to stop the user from having a narrow window and using a typeface like Desdemona:

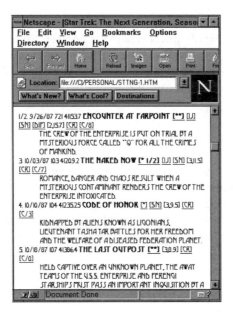

*Figure 2.2: A less likely, but possible, Netscape window*

### Freshness of information

When users pick up paper manuals, they can get a reasonable idea about how old the material is or how well-used it is by the condition of the cover and the pages. Dog-ears and coffee stains suggest something that is old (it may therefore be out of date) and well-used (the information is useful).

Screen-based information offers none of these clues. It always looks fresh and up to date, and it may not show any signs that someone has read it before. There is therefore pressure on the owner of the information to make sure that it is indeed kept up to date and that it clearly is useful information.

## Key points from the chapter

> - Make screen-based information as easy to read as possible
>
> - Structure information so that people don't have to jump about
>
> - Keep document length as short as possible so that users don't have to scroll too much
>
> - Provide good tools for navigation, such as indices and buttons to press
>
> - Concentrate on the content, not the cosmetics

# Chapter 3

# How to plan for success

# Chapter 3
## How to plan for success

After reading this chapter you will be able to:

- work with a customer to clarify what they want you to do

- name the team of people whom you will involve in the design project

- decide the best way to deliver the information

- prepare a project plan with dates for everyone involved

 ## What is the process?

Putting web-based information together calls for a project-based approach. You have to work through several separate stages to end up with a working web site, and it is important to go through each thoroughly. This will make sure that you build quality in to your site as you go along. Quality management for the design process in covered in more detail in Chapter 9.

| | |
|---|---|
| **Stage 1 – Planning** | First you must plan in general terms what information you need to provide, and how you will get it. This will probably involve other people, so you need to think about the different types of people you will need in your project team. |
| | You must think about what media you will use in addition to the intranet. For example, you may want to use e-mail to advertise the new site. |
| | You will need to put together a project plan. It need not be elaborate, and you may not need to draw up anything as sophisticated as a Gantt or Pert chart, but you should make some estimates about timescales and delivery dates. |
| | These issues are all covered in this chapter. |
| **Stage 2 – Drafting** | The next step is to prepare a first draft of your information using conventional paper-based techniques and word processor technology. |
| | These issues are covered in: |
| | • Chapter 4 – How to build a picture of your users |
| | • Chapter 5 – How to structure your materials |
| | • Chapter 6 – How to write your materials |

| | |
|---|---|
| **Stage 3 – Coding** | You must next think about your screen design, and choose colours, navigation, etc.<br><br>When you have done that, you can start to pour your text in to the pages.<br><br>This is covered in Chapter 7 – How to design your pages. |
| **Stage 4 – Testing** | I think it is important to identify testing as a separate stage, as it is vitally important. If your experience is mainly in paper-based information systems, you may not have had to do any software debugging, but that is one area you will have to explore here. Unlike paper, computer-based solutions can, and invariably do at the draft stage, fail to work properly.<br><br>It is also important at this stage to make sure that your end users are happy with the content.<br><br>Testing is looked at in Chapter 9 – How to make sure you develop a quality site. |
| **Stage 5 – Implementation** | When you have finished testing the site, you can set it up so that users can access it. You may need to advertise it, and you should also consider how you are going to keep an eye on how effective it is proving.<br><br>This is covered in Chapter 10 – How to check the success of your site. |

Having read the above, you may feel daunted by what you need to do. This is why it is important as a first step to plan ahead and work out what help you will need. This book will guide you through the basics of each of the stages.

The rest of this chapter looks at the planning stage. There are five steps involved here:

**1** Clarify the need

**2** Decide what approach to take

**3** Identify the key people involved

**4** Choose the correct media for delivery

**5** Develop a project plan

How to Design and Post Information on a Corporate Intranet

# 1 Clarify the need

The first thing to do when a customer asks you to design something for the intranet is to ask three simple questions:

> - Who is it for?
> - What are they doing at the moment?
> - What will you see as success?

**Why do you ask these questions?**

**Who is it for?**

This will start to clarify for you (and possibly the customer) who exactly is going to need this document. As we shall see, it is important when writing materials to be very clear about who is going to read it so that you can write for them.

The customer may say that it is for a specific group or groups of people. Make a note of who they are. They may say that it is for everybody. If that is their answer, you should push a little harder to find out exactly what they mean by that. Clarify:

- *Does everyone use this information the same amount, or do some use it daily while others use it once a year?*
- *Do all groups need exactly the same bits of information?*

Usually this will reveal that not everybody needs the same information. This is vital so that you can structure the intranet pages in ways that work for everybody.

**What are they doing at the moment?**

This will get you information on how the information is currently being delivered. Clarify:

- *Is this something new?*
- *Do they use reference manuals?*
- *Are there any problems with what they do at the moment? For example, do manuals get out of date? Do people make too many mistakes or take too much time?*

This information may be different for each group, so be prepared to probe.

**What will you see as success?**

This will encourage the customer to think about how they are going to measure the effectiveness of the information. This may be relatively easy to do, but this will not necessarily be the case. For example, if the material covers a routine procedure, it should be easy to measure success in terms of time savings and reductions in mistakes. However, if we are looking at something less tangible, such as a corporate mission statement, measures of success may be less tangible.

# 2 Decide what approach to take

What can vary enormously at this stage is the completeness of the information you are dealing with.  Consider these scenarios:

### Scenario 1

Customer: *'The board has just agreed the final wording to our statement on corporate values.  We want it to be available on the intranet.'*

### Scenario 2

Customer: *'I think the intranet would be a better way of delivering this information on safe manual handling procedures.  Can you do that for me?'*

### Scenario 3

Customer: *'We need some on-line guidance for our field surveyors on how to work out the energy efficiency of domestic properties.  We haven't got anything at the moment.'*

These scenarios range from having no scope at all for rewording through to starting from scratch.  The processes you can follow to put these on-line may therefore be somewhat different.  Think about these issues as you consider how to go about it.

| | |
|---|---|
| **You must write and structure material differently for an intranet.** | You must structure information more clearly, separate key information from that which is supplementary, and you will not find the same tolerance for excessive prose! |
| | So even if the task seems to be to simply add HTML code to an existing paper document, do not do it.  Go back to basics and follow the methods outlined in Chapter 5 for structuring the material.  Then map existing materials on to this structure, editing as necessary. |
| **Consider the measures of success for the material.** | For example, in Scenario 1 your customer may say that it will be a success if they can see people living the values.  Point out that you will have to add materials that relate those values to everyday tasks if this is to be achieved.  After all, how many people read a mission statement or declaration of values and really think about what that means for them in their everyday life? |
| | A statement of values is an excellent example of something that can be posted on an intranet, but if it is to have any measurable impact on the performances of individuals it must be supplemented by information on how to live by these values. |

| | |
|---|---|
| **What is the purpose of the information?** | All information should have a purpose. It should either be to:<br><br>• inform users about something, such as a policy statement<br>or:<br>• instruct someone in how to do something<br><br>The purpose will have a bearing on what approach to take. If it is to inform, you may need to take more care over its look and style. If it is to instruct, you will have to be much more careful about how it is structured. |
| **How complex do you want to make the site?** | As we shall see later in the book, there are various ways in which you can add complexity to your site. It can range from a simple site with basic graphics and HTML through to one with sophisticated Java programming and opportunities for the user to enter and extract data from database information.<br><br>The level of complexity you choose will depend on the resources you have available: do you have the people to program it, the money to pay them and the time for the development? |

We shall use these three scenarios throughout this book as case studies of how we can develop effective web-based information. In each chapter we shall work through the steps outlined here and see what we would do.

# 3 Identify the key people involved

Depending on the approach you are going to take for your materials, there are several different groups of people you may need to involve in the project. Some will be important in the early stages, while others will be more important later on in the development stage.

| | |
|---|---|
| **The customer** | This will probably be the person who asked you to do the work. They are important because you must get their approval for what you intend to do, and ultimately they will be the person who says that what you have done is acceptable.

Clarify with them what they will see as a sign of success for the project. Will this be fewer mistakes being made, less administrative time being spent, or savings on manual maintenance costs. Make these criteria as measurable as possible, as you will then be able to look back at them when the project has been implemented to see just how successful it has been. |
| **The high performers** | High performers do the job quickly with the minimum of effort and can show you how they do it. Do not assume that high performers will be senior people in the organisation – they will be at the level that uses this information (or part of the information) the most. If, for example, we were looking at providing information on completing travel expense claims, we could first talk to a person who processes expense claims. Ask them for the names of people who fill in their forms accurately, and those who never leave gaps or put in ambiguous information. |
| **The subject matter expert** | These are the people who know everything about the subject. They will be useful later in the design process, but can be dangerous to involve right at the start. With their possible enthusiasm for the subject, you run the risk of having a lot of superfluous information in your on-line information. For example, they may think the user needs to know all about relevant legislation, the reasons for the job being done this way, and so on. Remembering that people usually find it harder to absorb a lot of information from a screen than from paper. You need to present information clearly and concisely, so too much information may make your site less effective.

The time to draw on your subject matter expert is when you have prepared a first draft of the content. Let the expert read through it so they can check to see that your material is factually correct. The subject matter expert should be the person who actually signs the material off as correct, so you may need to consider whether they have enough authority within your organisation to do this. |

| | |
|---|---|
| **The end users** | Involve end users right from the start.  Before you start on the design, you might need to ask them, for example, what: <br><br>• they know about the subject <br>• they find difficult <br>• they do not like about the information they have at present <br><br>During the testing stage they can tell you whether your language is clear, whether they find the hyperlinks a help or a hindrance, and whether they find the material practical enough for them to want to use it.  Failing to involve users in the design process can mean that you design beautiful on-line information that nobody uses. |
| **The information owner** | This is the person who is going to take responsibility for looking after the site once it has been implemented.  It may be the customer or the subject matter expert, but it may be you, even if you do not realise it now! <br><br>Clarify who is going to own the information before you start, so that you can think about how the site will be updated. |

# 4 Choose the correct media for delivery

It is at this point that we must look at the material in question and make some decisions about the best way of presenting the information. Is it going to be enough to post it on the intranet, or should we advertise it using other media? It is also important to ask whether or not it should go on the intranet in the first place.

One of the key concepts that the use of an intranet introduces is that of moving from an information-push to an information-pull culture. Traditionally organisations push information at employees, even if they do not need it, as there may be no simple way of filtering out who does from who does not. That leads to potentially huge wastes of effort and money. An intranet allows individuals to pull out what information they need, potentially saving a lot of time and effort. It also implies a more adult view of employees, in that they can make their own decisions about what they need.

You will probably be using several different ways of delivering information to your users. Each of them has advantages and disadvantages. The most important media are:

- intranet reference – permanently available

- intranet journals – posted for a few weeks then removed

- e-mail

- paper documents

- posters and flyers

- presentations

This table summarises some of the issues you need to consider when deciding which medium to use.

| Medium | Good for: | Not so good for: |
|---|---|---|
| **Intranet reference** | • standard procedures that people always need<br>• reference documents<br>• information that changes frequently<br>• information that not everybody needs<br>• information that links in with other related information sources | • transient information<br>• material needing immediate replies from people<br>• instances where you need to be sure that everyone has seen the information<br>• lengthy pieces of text (say over 2500 words)<br>• anything requiring careful, analytical thought<br>• confidential information<br>• video or sound (although theoretically possible, it is technically difficult at the moment)<br>• detailed graphical information (e.g. illustrations, plans) |

| Medium | Good for: | Not so good for: |
|---|---|---|
| **Intranet journals** | • topical information<br>• information about new developments, policies, procedures, etc.<br>• advertising what is happening on the intranet | • longer-term information<br>• video or sound<br>• highly detailed graphical information (for example illustrations, plans) |
| **E-mail** | • information with a very short shelf-life, e.g. requests to complete specific returns by a certain date in the near future<br>• information sent to a small number of people<br>• confidential information | • any form of reference |
| **Paper** | • instances where you must be sure that everyone within a specific group receives the information, such as major organisational changes<br>• longer passages of text, where there is a need to analyse the information<br>• material with complex graphics | • instances where information is going to be needed for some time but is subject to continual changes |
| **Posters and flyers** | • catching people's attention<br>• clear signpost of something new | • making sure people actually stop to read them<br>• organisations where there are a lot of posters and flyers! |
| **Presentations** | • making sure you know who has and who has not received the information<br>• times where you need to allow face-to-face dialogue | • issues where it is not clear who needs to be targeted, so a blanket approach has to be taken<br>• relatively small issues which do not warrant taking people away from their desks<br>• ensuring complete consistency of delivery |

It is likely that you will decide to use several different media for different purposes. For example, a major organisational policy initiative may need a site on the intranet, with publicity through e-mails, posters and presentations. Smaller projects may only require a brief article in the intranet journal giving the URL and an entry in a What's New section.

# 5 Develop a project plan

It is beyond the scope of this book to cover the subject of project management. What we will do is look at the steps you should take to make sure each of your projects can be a success.

| | |
|---|---|
| **Clarify expectations with the customer** | Arrange a meeting(s) where you:<br><br>• get a clear statement about what the customer will see as a successful project<br><br>• prepare a list of names of people to work on the project, with a statement about what their responsibilities will be, i.e. high performers, subject matter experts<br><br>• agree the budget in time and money available<br><br>• agree desired dates for each stage of the project, i.e.:<br>  • prototype<br>  • first draft<br>  • completion of alpha testing<br>  • completion of beta testing<br>  • implementation<br><br>• media for delivery<br><br>• strategy for implementation, advertising for example, if necessary |
| **Estimate timescales** | Estimate how long it will take to work through each stage of the process. These stages are:<br><br>• development of standards for the project (which may already be defined organisation-wide)<br><br>• research to gather information<br><br>• preparing the first draft of a prototype of the design with part of the project<br><br>• checking the prototype with the project team and making necessary edits<br><br>• designing the remainder of the project<br><br>• carrying out alpha testing with user groups and making edits<br><br>• carrying out beta testing with user groups and making edits<br><br>• having the material proofread<br><br>• getting final approval from the customer |

Work these out in terms of days and then see how this fits in with the calendar and your customer's expectations. You may find that you need to bring some extra resources in to the design stage to speed that up or to renegotiate timescales with your customer.

Your ability to estimate how long it will take to carry out each of these stages will improve with experience, but there are some tips you will find useful:

- allow time at each stage to follow your quality assurance procedures

- allow as much time for the testing phases as for the design phase – not spending enough time testing materials is the single most likely cause of project failure

- allow twice as much time for proofreading an on-line document as a paper-based version, for reasons discussed earlier.

- allow a week at least for beta testing

| | |
|---|---|
| **Agree milestone dates with the project team** | When you have finished estimating timescales, see what these mean in terms of those dates where key people need to set aside time. Agree with them that they will need to be available on these dates to work on the project. Do not leave this to the last minute, or they will not be able to get the work done properly. |

# What are the case studies in this book?

We shall look at each of the scenarios and see how we could tackle the steps discussed in the chapter.

> **Scenario 1**
> Customer: *'The board has just agreed the final wording to our statement on corporate values. We want it to be available on the intranet.'*

| Step 1 – Clarify the need | Ask your customer the three questions: |
|---|---|
| | *'Who is it for?'* |
| | 'Well, it's for everyone in the company. But different people will want different things out of it. |
| | Line managers will want to know how it affects the way they manage their staff. Different departments will find some values of more importance than others. For example, providing a quality service means more to our sales staff than to estates, although it is obviously still of importance.' |
| | *'What are they doing at the moment?'* |
| | 'We've got some very good people out there, who already place a lot of importance in what these values say. But on the whole it's a mixed bag. |
| | The biggest problem is probably people not seeing other departments in the company as being customers. They don't see that we are supposed to work as a team.' |
| | *'What will you see as success?'* |
| | 'I suppose it will be a success if I could go into any office and see examples of people actually living out these values. But that is a big task, and I don't expect just writing these values out and publicising them will make that happen. But it's a start.' |
| **Step 2 – Decide what approach to take** | The first, and most obvious, step is to take the values statement, work out an attractive page design and publish it on the web. But you will also have to think about publicising it. |
| | The fact that different levels of managers and different departments will have varying types of interest in the values suggests that you could explore in more detail what these are. The values statement will interest people if they can see how to apply it in their everyday work, so you may want to think about trying to capture some best practice and publicising that. |

| | |
|---|---|
| **Step 3 – Identify the key people involved** | If you want to give users some information on best practice, you will need to go and find some high performers. Look at each value, and try to put one or two names against each. You can then go and ask them how they put these values into practice.<br><br>Identify some departments that have a particular interest in each value, and that are thought to be living them out. Talk to the heads of that department and find out what they do.<br><br>Talk also to the end users. Show them the values statement and see what their reactions are. What would make them find it a useful document? |
| **Step 4 – Choose the correct media for delivery** | You may well think that there are a number of ways in which you could deliver this information, in addition to putting it on the intranet:<br><br>• Write an article about it for an on-line journal.<br><br>• Design some posters that you can put up in key areas of the building, places where people stop and stare, such as lifts and canteen queuing areas.<br><br>• Prepare some presentation material for line managers so that they can run a short session explaining the values to their teams. |
| **Step 5 – Develop a project plan** | When you have thought about what you want to do, discuss your ideas with the customer. You should have some good information about possible user reaction that would be valuable if they are sceptical of your ideas.<br><br>If they think you are right, you can go ahead and start to prepare an action plan involving your high performers, with timescales and milestones. |

| | |
| :--- | :--- |
| **Step 1 – Clarify the need** | *'Who is it for?'*<br>'Everybody needs to know how to lift properly. Time off due to back problems is expensive, and we also need to satisfy the inspectors that we are carrying out our statutory responsibilities.<br><br>But there are some staff, such as maintenance, that are lifting all the time and they may need some extra information.'<br><br>*'What are they doing at the moment?'*<br>'We lose about 300 people-days due to back problems a year. People know how to lift properly but they just don't do it.'<br><br>*'What will you see as success?'*<br>'I would like to see everybody following the rules and using the right equipment. Also, if we could cut the time lost to back problems I would be very happy.' |
| **Step 2 – Decide what approach to take** | You can start off by looking at the existing information and thinking about how to reword and restructure it.<br><br>You may want to talk to the head of maintenance and see if they have any special needs.<br><br>Also think about the fact that people know how to lift properly but don't do it. Why? People may find information on the implications of back problems more powerful than information on safe lifting procedures. |
| **Step 3 – Identify the key people involved** | You will want to talk to the head of maintenance and also people in your occupational health department. Experienced people in maintenance will be able to talk to you about real-life lifting problems and how they deal with them. The may also have personal accounts of back pain. |
| **Step 4 – Choose the correct media for delivery** | Lifting is a skill, something that people do rather than know about, so the best way to improve performance is by letting people practise. You could therefore see if you can organise practice sessions run by suitable staff for small groups of people.<br><br>Supplement this with a poster campaign. |
| **Step 5 – Develop a project plan** | As before, discuss your ideas with the customer, and if they are happy, start putting a plan together. |

| Step 1 – Clarify the need | *'Who is it for?'*<br>'It's for our field staff who have to carry out property surveys.'<br><br>*'What are they doing at the moment?'*<br>'This is a new area for them. None of them has done it before.'<br><br>*'What will you see as success?'*<br>'They have to be accredited by the Buildings Research Establishment assessors. I would like to see all of them as being accredited within six months.' |
| :--- | :--- |
| **Step 2 – Decide what approach to take** | This is new material, so you will have to develop some training materials. This could be based around checklists of each step the surveyor has to take, supplemented by some self-assessment questions. |
| **Step 3 – Identify the key people involved** | As this is a new area, you may not have the expertise in-house, in which case you will need to talk to one of the assessors to find out where you can get the information. |
| **Step 4 – Choose the correct media for delivery** | You may find that paper is more suitable as a delivery medium for the surveyors if the subject turns out to require some complex thought and analysis.<br><br>However, if it turns out to be a simple procedure and the surveyors are familiar with using computers, the intranet could be a very effective way of delivering the training. If they use portable computers on-site, you could even adapt the training so that the surveyors enter the data while following the on-screen information. |
| **Step 5 – Develop a project plan** | Once you have found out about the procedures, you can make some estimates about timescales and prepare your project plan. |

# Key points from the chapter

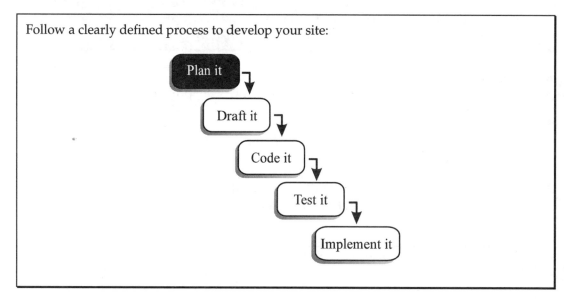

Follow a clearly defined process to develop your site:

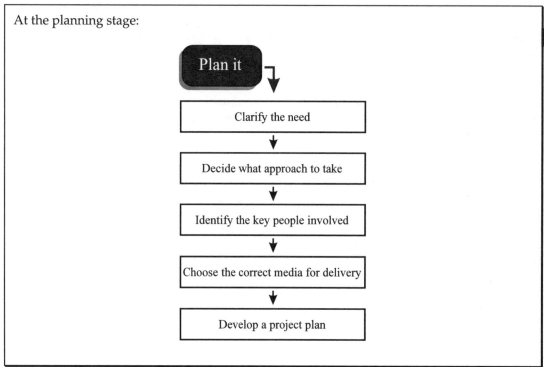

At the planning stage:

# Chapter

# How to build a picture of your users

How to Design and Post Information on a Corporate Intranet

# Chapter 4
## How to build a picture of your users

After reading this chapter you will be able to:

- describe what your typical user is like

One of the key principles to follow in any sort of writing is to write with someone in mind. That applies as much on an intranet as anywhere. If, while you are writing, you think about the people who will be reading it, you can pitch the language at the right level and avoid making people feel they are being patronised, or that the material is going over their heads. You can include just the right amount of professional jargon and avoid analogies and idioms that are inappropriate. For example, how appropriate are male sporting analogies such as 'kicking off' to a largely female audience? You can decide whether to include definitions and explanations of important concepts within the body of the text, which would be useful for newcomers, or to separate it out and offer it as optional material at the end of a hyperlink, which would be better for users who know the subject well.

One of the big advantages that intranet delivery has over paper is that you can structure materials so that all users see a 'basic' version, and more complex or explanatory material is available through a hyperlink. This is a way of providing several reading levels, with the user able to choose which they are interested in.

What are the steps to follow?

 Draw up a list of users

Prepare a profile of them

# Draw up a list of users

Work with your project team to develop a list of all the groups of people who are going to use the materials. We shall call these people your target groups. If there are many different groups or grades, try to simplify them into two or three general categories. For example, you might have some material that is only of interest to one particular grade, and it should be relatively straightforward to build a picture of a typical job holder. On the other hand, some materials will be used by everyone. Then it may be more practicable to categorise people as, perhaps, clerical, middle managers and senior managers.

We shall refer to these categories of people as 'target groups'.

# Prepare a profile

For each group, get a sheet of flip chart paper. On it draw a large outline of a person. Do not worry about the level of artistic skill – a matchstick person is fine for this.

On each one, write down observations about:

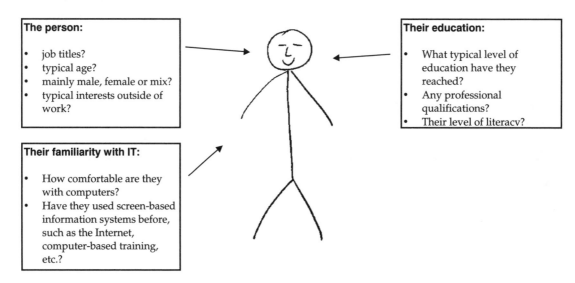

*Figure 4.1: What to look for in your target group*

This exercise will help you to think about what assumptions you can make about what they can do, how well they can read, etc. Keep this picture in mind when you start writing.

How to Design and Post Information on a Corporate Intranet

# Who are the target groups in the case studies?

**Scenario 1**

Customer: *'The board has just agreed the final wording to our statement on corporate values. We want it to be available on the intranet.'*

| Step 1 | This is an example of where everyone will need to read the main values statement, so this will need to have been written with a very average audience in mind. Given the hours of debate that may have gone in to the exact phrasing of such a document, you may not have any scope at all for changing the original wording. |
|---|---|
| | Such documents often use quite sophisticated adjectives, so you will need to test the original document out on a cross-section of employees and find out where people find it difficult to understand. You can then use the hyperlinking ability of the intranet to build in extra information that some users may want. |
| | You could decide here to add some extra information for typical line managers who would be interested in knowing how the values statement will affect their managerial styles. |
| Step 2 | As the wording of the values statement is fixed, you could decide not to spend time developing a profile for this general group. Instead, look at the profile of a typical line manager: |

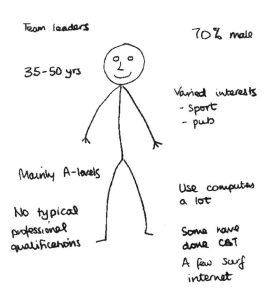

Figure 4.2: A profile of a typical line manager

**Scenario 2**
Customer: *'I think the intranet would be a better way of delivering this information on safe manual handling procedures. Can you do that for me?'*

**Step 1**

You think that there may be two levels of information here, a basic level for all staff and an advanced level for maintenance staff. The material you write for all staff will need to be aimed at a very general audience, while you can be more focused for the advanced level material.

**Step 2**

The general audience is something like this:

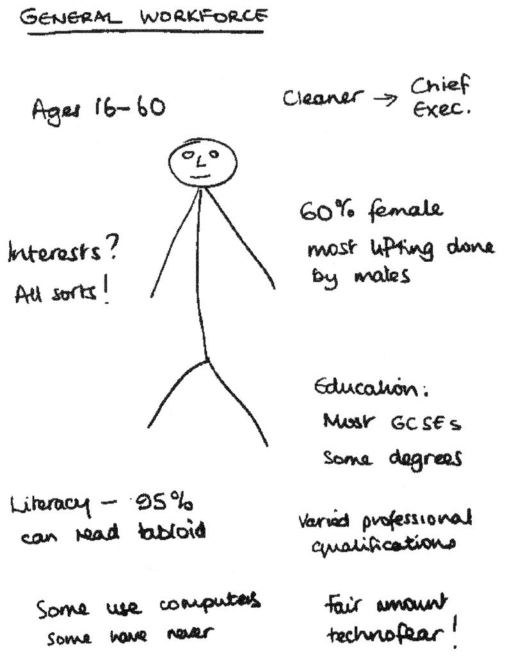

GENERAL WORKFORCE
Ages 16-60
Cleaner → Chief Exec.
60% female
most lifting done by males
Interests? All sorts!
Education: Most GCSEs Some degrees
Literacy – 95% can read tabloid
Varied professional qualifications
Some use computers Some have never
Fair amount technofear!


*Figure 4.3: The profile of the overall target group*

The typical maintenance person is more like this:

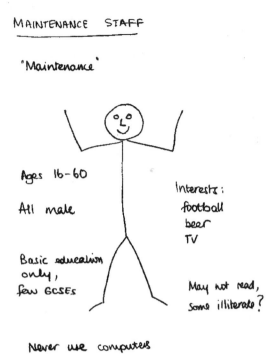

MAINTENANCE STAFF

"Maintenance"

Ages 16-60

All male

Basic education
only,
few GCSEs

Interests:
football
beer
TV

May not read,
some illiterate?

Never use computers

*Figure 4.4: A profile of a typical maintenance person*

This profile suggests that any computer-based delivery will need to be easy to use so that people can pick it up. A graphical approach would also help to get around the problem of limited literacy.

You may also want to ask at this stage whether these staff do in fact have access to a computer, and if not, whether developing special intranet-based material for them is appropriate.

Scenario 3
Customer: *'We need some on-line guidance for our field surveyors on how to work out the energy efficiency of domestic properties. We haven't got anything at the moment.'*

| | |
|---|---|
| **Step 1** | This is a simple case here: there is one clearly defined target group, the surveyors. |
| **Step 2** | Surveyors are in general: |

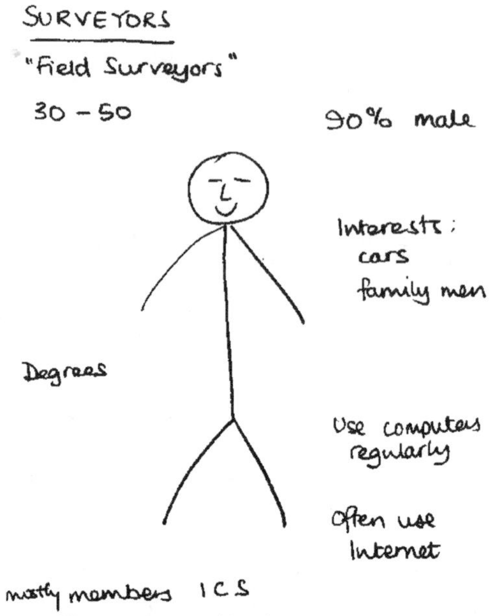

SURVEYORS
"Field Surveyors"
30 – 50
90% male
Interests:
cars
family men
Degrees
Use computers regularly
Often use Internet
mostly members ICS


Figure 4.5: A profile of a typical surveyor

They are a well-defined group of educated individuals who are probably going to be comfortable with the intranet as an information source.

# Key points from the chapter

- Work out who are the people who will be using your site.
- Write with this target group in mind.

# Chapter

5

# How to structure your materials

# Chapter 5
## How to structure your materials

After reading this chapter you will be able to:

> • decide on an appropriate way or ways to break down the subject matter
>
> • break down a procedural task into separate sub-tasks

 ## What are the methods?

The key to the design of effective information on a web site lies in its structure. It is relatively easy to take paper-based materials, add HTML code and post them on a web site, but if information is to be effective you must take great care over its structure. You can present paper-based materials to a user and, because of the relative ease of handling paper, they can manipulate the information they need. This is not so easy with on-screen information, so as a designer you must work out how to break the material down into manageable 'chunks'. Doing this properly is probably the hardest part of the whole web site design process.

The secret is to step back from the detail and ask the question: 'What will the user want to do with this information?' If you cannot think of a good answer for that, ask some typical users. If they cannot think of a good answer either, you may want to review whether or not you should spend any time designing it at all!

There are a number of techniques we can use when trying to develop a structure for intranet materials. We shall look at three of them, each of which you might want to use in different circumstances. These are:

| Key words | The material contains obvious key words or phrases, from which we can make a hyperlink that takes the user on to explore something about that word or phrase. |
|---|---|
| Frequently Asked Questions (FAQ) | Anyone who has used the Internet will recognise this technique. There are, for most subjects, a number of questions that users of the information often ask. Hyperlinks attached to these questions lead on to answers and perhaps more questions. |
| Pyramid analysis | This is the most rigorous of the three, and is useful when the material is of a procedural nature. It is very powerful when you need to break down a task into a sequence of sub-tasks in a logical order. |

We shall look at each of these techniques in turn, and see how we can apply them to our case studies. It is important to recognise that they are not exclusive, and you may find that a combination works well. For example, you might use a key word approach to give an initial structure to a document, then offer some FAQs about each word, then use pyramid analysis to give some procedural information in your answer to each question.

Recognise that what you are doing is creating something, like an artist. With art there is a spectrum of representation that ranges from completely abstract through to almost photographic quality. Designing content for a web site is something like that. You will have some content that needs an impressionistic touch, and for which there is no right or wrong structure. Other content, such as clearly defined procedural information, requires an exact representation. If you are not sure about how to move forward on a design, remember that the best design is the one the user finds most useful.

The nature of the medium makes it relatively easy to try different ideas out and test them with the users. You do not necessarily have to have just one structure. You can also design hyperlinks so that there may be more than one way of accessing the information.

How to Design and Post Information on a Corporate Intranet

# Method 1 – Key words

This is useful for text that is meant to inform rather than instruct, such as policy documents, journal articles, etc. To see how we might use it, let us look at Scenario 1, the values statement.

Here is our values statement:

## Wonderwidgets Plc
### *Our values*

At Wonderwidgets we value:

**personal development** – we all have a chance to develop in ways that maximise our sense of personal fulfilment and that contribute to the success of the business; achieving this through planned training and development activities.

**exceeding customers' expectations** – we always look for ways to go the extra mile for internal and external customers; being right first time, accurate and punctual.

**innovation** – we continuously look for new ways of using our expertise in new and successful ways, through harnessing the power of new technology, improving flexibility in work patterns; supporting this at all levels by encouraging initiative and offering appropriate rewards.

**teamwork** – we work together as a team, using the synergy of combining our many talents to improve ourselves as individuals and as an organisation.

**openness** – we share with colleagues our hopes, fears and frustrations, so that our working relationships are conducted on an adult level; offering constructive feedback when requested in an atmosphere of trust.

**taking responsibility** – we look for opportunities to increase our own levels of responsibility and to find ways of increasing those of reporting staff; ensuring responsibility with power.

*Figure 5.1: The Wonderwidgets values statement*

Fine words, but what would it mean to people at Wonderwidgets? What would make this of more than passing interest to them?

## Ask them and find out

We can find out what the key words are by a brainstorming exercise. There are various ways of running brainstorming sessions that you may have used before and they may be suitable here. This method is one that I have found to be effective as a way of encouraging participation from even the most timid person, as it lets the participants think about the text on their own in silence.

To do this exercise you will need:

- 10 pads of 76 x 127 mm Post-it® notes
- 10 marker pens
- a flip chart or wall
- some means of displaying the values statement to a group (hand-written on a flip chart or with an overhead projector, for example)

When you have these ready:

1. Gather together between 5 and 10 members of your target group.

2. Give each participant a pad of Post-it® notes and a marker pen.

3. Display the statement to the group.

4. Ask people to read through the statement and write on a Post-it® any word or phrase that they find powerful or that they do not really understand.

5. Allow about five minutes for them to do this, but do not stop people if they are still writing enthusiastically at the end of this time.

6. When everyone has finished writing, ask each person in turn to stick up on the flip chart or wall what they have written as being powerful. They do not need to justify it in any way.

7. When everyone has finished, work with the group to sort the words and phrases. Look for duplicates and identify the most powerful items. There could be between three and six of these as a guess, depending on the length and complexity of the statement.

8. Repeat this process for the words or phrases that they do not really understand.

Look at how this could work for the case study:

**Scenario 1**
Customer: 'The board has just agreed the final wording to our statement on corporate values. We want it to be available on the intranet.'

If we did this for the Wonderwidgets values statement we might end up with something like this:

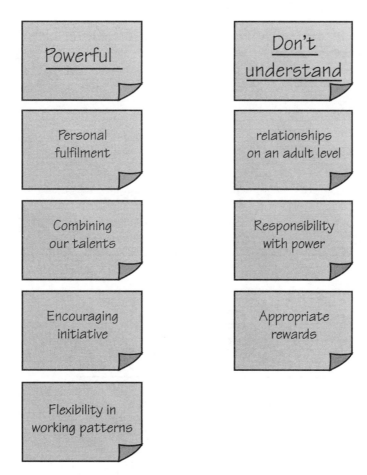

*Figure 5.2: Key words from the values statement*

**Explore these key words**

When you have identified these key words, you can repeat the brainstorming process for each of them in turn:

1. Taking the first key word as an example, write 'Personal fulfilment' on a Post-it® and put it at the top of your sheet of flip chart paper.

2. Ask the group to write on their Post-its® what they want to know about that key word or what it makes them think about.

3. When they are all ready, get each person to stick up their Post-its®.

4. Repeat this for each key word.

Looking at this for the case study:

**Scenario 1**
Customer: *'The board has just agreed the final wording to our statement on corporate values. We want it to be available on the intranet.'*

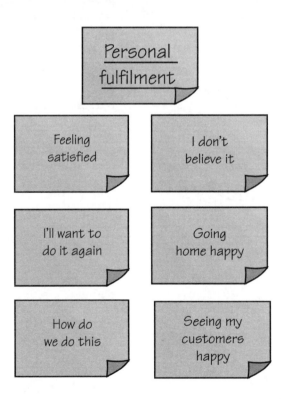

*Figure 5.3: Exploring the key words*

**Plan your content**

You now use these statements to work out what you can put on the web site. This should prove to be useful for people in the organisation, as we have found out what a typical group of users feels about the information, and what they would like to see to flesh it out. Do not feel that you have to include everything that people have said: use their responses as a guide only.

In the case study:

---

**Scenario 1**
Customer: *'The board has just agreed the final wording to our statement on corporate values. We want it to be available on the intranet.'*

---

For example, looking at the responses above suggests the following:

- Something describing how people feel when they are fulfilled

- Things you can do to work towards a sense of personal fulfilment

- What some people are doing to help them achieve it

- Titles of books that people could read about fulfilment

- Training available that could help someone achieve fulfilment, such as customer care training

If you now went ahead and designed information around these possibilities, you would feel more confident that it would be what users were actually going to be interested in.

# Method 2 – Frequently asked questions

You have probably seen paper-based information sources where headings are written as questions, such as: 'Where do I send my completed form?' This technique is used extensively on the Internet for offering information. For example, look at this page from the Netscape site:

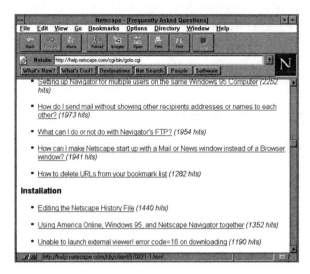

*Figure 5.4: Examples of Frequently Asked Questions*

Internet jargon calls this technique the Frequently Asked Question, or FAQ, so we shall use that term here.

While it is a useful technique for someone looking for information, it can be difficult for you as a designer to know just what a frequently asked question might be, especially if you have no involvement in the particular subject. On the other hand, if you are knowledgeable about the subject, you will probably have forgotten what a newcomer does not understand and wants to know. What I therefore suggest is that you go out ask people what they want to know about the subject. That gives you your FAQs!

There are some potential drawbacks to the FAQ approach that you need to be aware of:

- If the subject is completely new, people may not know what they want to know. From the designer's perspective this can make it difficult to generate useful questions.

- Again, with a new subject, a user may not know what question they should be asking.

- A user with a specific query may not see a question that corresponds to it, so that they cannot find the information they need.

You can combine this approach with the other techniques described in this chapter. For example, in our case study:

> **Scenario 1**
> Customer: *'The board has just agreed the final wording to our statement on corporate values. We want it to be available on the intranet.'*

You could convert any of the ideas produced in the previous section into an FAQ:

- How will I feel when I am fulfilled?
- What can I do to work towards a sense of personal fulfilment?
- What are other people are doing to help them achieve fulfilment?
- What books are there around that I could read?
- What training is available that could help me?

## How can I generate some FAQs?

You can use the same process as in Method 1 for generating ideas for FAQs. Get your users to do the hard work for you.

One thing to remember with this approach is that if you advertise questions as 'frequently asked', you should check to see that they remain so. If you do not, your information can lose credibility. Investigate ways of keeping up to date with what people want to know about the subject so that you can keep your site alive and relevant. Chapter 10 looks at ways you can do this.

# Method 3 – Pyramid analysis

The first two methods work well for more abstract material, but if you are looking to find ways of presenting procedural information you will need to use a more rigorous approach. The method I shall describe here is an application of a technique used in training design, where it is called 'task' or 'pyramid analysis'. This is because you end up with a pyramid of tasks, several at the bottom leading up to a single one at the top, the overall objective.

It is actually a three-step process:

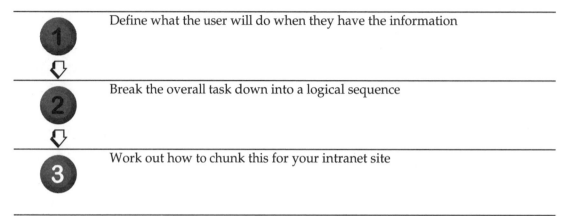

| | |
|---|---|
| 1 | Define what the user will do when they have the information |
| 2 | Break the overall task down into a logical sequence |
| 3 | Work out how to chunk this for your intranet site |

We can now look at these steps in more detail.

**Define what the user must do**

The first thing you must do is work out what a user will be able do to when they have followed the information. You do this by writing an objective.

The word 'objective' can mean many different things. It is often confused with 'aims', for example. Here we shall be looking at it from a training perspective and be using it in a fairly technical way. We will define it as:

> *what you can see a person doing, incorporating a measure of success*

Training textbooks offer different definitions of what an objective is, and provide more or less rigorous ways in which they should be written. You may well have come across the idea of the SMART objective, which stipulates that an objective must be:

- Specific
- Measurable
- Achievable
- Realistic
- Timebound

Other approaches suggest writing an objective with four parts:

- Conditions, under which the performance is carried out
- Performance, that the person can be watched doing
- Standards of success, how well they carry out the performance
- Assessment method, how we can check to see that they have carried the performance out successfully

These methods are important if you are designing training materials, but for your purposes you can simplify them into something more workable, with just a performance and a measure of success.

Look at these examples:

| Objective | Comment |
|---|---|
| *Fry an egg so that the white has set and the yolk is still runny* | You can watch someone fry an egg, and most people would define it as successful if the yolk is still runny! |
| *Change a car tyre within 15 minutes* | You can watch someone change a car tyre and 15 minutes is a reasonable time within which to do it. |
| *Know how a browser works* | You cannot watch someone know something. Also, how well do they know it? People have knowledge in order to do something, so we could rewrite this as:<br><br>*Describe how a browser works so that they agree with information provided in Chapter 1 of this book.* |

You can work out what your objective should be by talking to your customer and high performers. They will tell you what the real performance is and how you can tell if you are doing it successfully. See how this works in our case studies:

> **Scenario 1**
> Customer: *'The board has just agreed the final wording to our statement on corporate values. We want it to be available on the intranet.'*

The customer said they would see it as a sign of success if 'I could go into any office and see examples of people actually living out these values'. We therefore need to look at the values and think about what someone who was living the values could be seen doing. For example, they might:

- share feelings with colleagues so that colleagues say they always feel clear about their relationship

- give responsibility to colleagues so that these people have the necessary authority and are comfortable

You probably think these are very woolly, and you are right. Designing objectives for 'touchy-feely' subjects like this is very difficult. If you wanted to design a training programme about how to share feelings with colleagues, you would, none the less, have to do it. In this case, you would probably decide at this stage that pyramid analysis is not a very appropriate method.

> **Scenario 2**
> Customer: *'I think the intranet would be a better way of delivering this information on safe manual handling procedures. Can you do that for me?'*

The customer said they would like to 'see everybody following the rules and using the right equipment'. It is easier to define an objective here. It would probably be something like:

- lift any object using the appropriate method and equipment, so that you follow the recommended procedure

This presupposes that there is a 'recommended procedure'. This in itself should have as its objective that people following it will not injure themselves.

> **Scenario 3**
> Customer: *'We need some on-line guidance for our field surveyors on how to work out the energy efficiency of domestic properties. We haven't got anything at the moment.'*

The customer's measure of success is that all the surveyors 'have to be accredited by the Buildings Research Establishment assessors. I would like to see all of them as being accredited within six months.' That is a very clear standard for the surveyors to meet. Your objective would therefore be to:

- assess a property to the satisfaction of a Buildings Research Establishment assessor within six months

**Break the performance down**

Once you have defined the objective you need to break it down to see what separate tasks have to be completed in order to achieve it. For example, what separate tasks do you have to do in order to fry an egg so that the yolk is still runny?

This is where we use pyramid analysis. It is a very simple technique, but it does need practice before you can feel comfortable about doing it. Essentially what you do is to ask the question 'What do you have to do in order to do that?' over and over again, applying it first to the overall objective then to the sub-tasks that come out of this.

Let us examine the process in more detail.

---

You will need:

- your high performer(s)
- a large wall or flip chart
- a few pads of small Post-it® notes (the 38 x 51 mm size)

---

1. Write the overall objective at the top of the flip chart page.

2. Ask the high performer(s) the question: 'What do you have to do in order to achieve this objective?'

3. Write whatever they say on a Post-it® and stick it on the flip chart underneath the objective.

4. Ask them what they have to do in order to do that.

5. Write their answer down and stick that underneath the previous Post-it®.

6. Repeat this for each task that they tell you about, exploring each sub-task in turn, then going back and exploring other tasks that must be carried out in order to achieve the objective.

7. Carry on until your high performers think they have completely described the task.

This shows how the process works for Scenario 2:

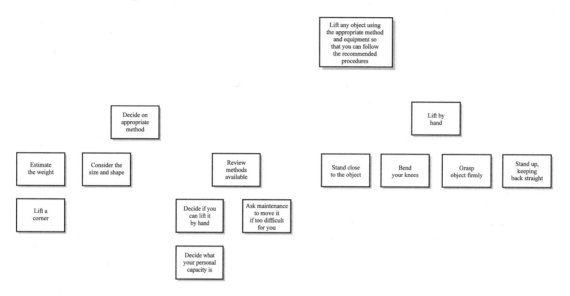

*Figure 5.5: Pyramid analysis for a safe manual load handling procedure*

This may look quite straightforward, but in reality the questioning process may have been fairly complicated. The conversation to get to this stage may go something like this:

| | |
|---|---|
| Designer | 'What do you have to do in order to lift any object using the appropriate method?' |
| HP | 'First of all you have to decide how to lift it.' |
| Designer | 'How do you do that?' |
| HP | 'You see how heavy it is.' |
| Designer | 'How do you do that?' |
| HP | 'Well, you see if you can lift a corner up.' |
| Designer | 'Then what?' |
| HP | 'You decide whether it is too heavy for you or not.' |
| Designer | 'What about the shape of it? Does that make any difference?' |
| HP | 'Oh yes. You have to think about that as well.' |
| Designer | 'OK. So you estimate the weight by lifting a corner, then you think about whether it is an easy size and shape, then you decide what to do. Is that right?' |
| HP | 'Yes, if you decide you can't lift it, then you'd call someone from maintenance to move it.' |
| Designer | 'Let's assume that it is OK. What do you do?' |
| HP | 'Well, you bend your knees, grab hold of it then lift. You've got to make sure you keep your back straight.' |
| Designer | 'You probably need to get as close to the object as possible, I guess.' |
| HP | 'Yes, you'd do that first.' |

And so on. The finished pyramid looks very straightforward, but getting to it may not be quite so easy. See how the high performer may not tell you everything in the right order, and you will need to think about what they say and how it all fits together. This is the beauty of using Post-it® notes: you can move them around until they do make sense.

There are some guidelines to follow when doing a pyramid analysis:

| | |
|---|---|
| **Make the first word on every Post-it® a watchable verb** | When you are writing out the Post-its®, make sure that the first word on each one describes an action you can see. Avoid the invisible actions of knowing and understanding. If that is what your high performer tells you they do, probe until they tell you what they actually do with that knowledge or understanding: that is what you are interested in. |
| **Recognise when to stop** | If you carry on analysing relentlessly, you will end up with actions such as breathe, wake up in the morning, etc. These will probably seem ridiculous, so one thing you must decide is at what level to stop.<br><br>You decide this on the basis of what you expect your target group to be able to do already. For example, for the action 'Grasp object firmly', you would not expect to have to explain how to do that to adults and you would therefore stop developing this line of the pyramid here. However, if you were trying to explain to a three year old child you may well need to explain how you do grasp an object firmly. |
| **Allow yourself to be confused** | Do not expect everything to come out in exactly the right order. People do not generally think in very logical ways about jobs they are familiar with. You will therefore get sub-tasks coming out before main tasks.<br><br>Look out for this happening and test it by asking the question: 'What do I have to do in order to ...?' The logic of the answers to this question will allow you to sort the Post-its® into the right order. |
| **Look out for tasks that are substantial subjects in their own right** | You will often come across sub-tasks that are complex in themselves but it seems that to explore them would take you into areas of little relevance to the performance you are looking at. For example, in the pyramid above, you could have decided that reviewing the lifting methods available meant that you started looking at trolley technology.<br><br>This is clearly not of relevance here, so if you think that it is important that the user understands about this, you can tell them to go off and find some information elsewhere. In training jargon, it is a *prerequisite* to this information.<br><br>The interest of this to us when designing a web site is that you can make such prerequisite information available to the user through a hyperlink. You could set the page up so that if someone really wants to learn about trolley technology they could go away and look at it, then come back to the main body of information. |

| Test your pyramid out with other people | Good pyramids evolve. They start out as a tangle of disconnected Post-its® then slowly metamorphose into an accurate picture of the whole performance. This can only happen if you work through it with several people.

So go through your pyramid with your high performers to see that they agree with the logic of it. |
| --- | --- |

Notice that up until now you have relied on high performers rather than subject matter experts. This is because the high performers will give you the essential information you need. Involve the subject matter expert when you have a working pyramid. They will be able to see whether there is anything crucial missing or if there is anything technically wrong.

If the subject matter expert does want you to add extra material, make sure that this material is important to the process. However, once again the flexibility created by hyperlinking can be useful. If the material is not essential to the performance but is useful to have available, you can add it as a hyperlink off the main flow of information. Unlike with paper-based delivery, the user does not have to go through everything.

## Chunk the material

You have seen how to take a simple task such as lifting a heavy object and use pyramid analysis to break it down into simple sub-tasks. In this next step we shall see how using the technique at higher levels of performance automatically breaks the performance down into 'chunks', the term web designers use to describe the packet of information that comes on each page. This will generate the overall structure of the site.

Look at how pyramid analysis works for the objective in Scenario 3:

**Scenario 3**
Customer: *'We need some on-line guidance for our field surveyors on how to work out the energy efficiency of domestic properties. We haven't got anything at the moment.'*

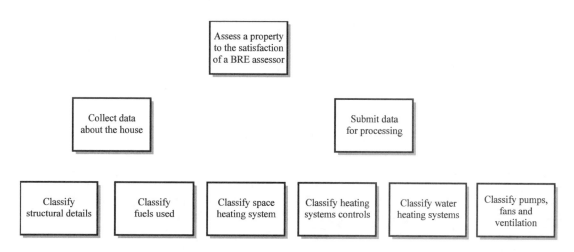

*Figure 5.6: Overall procedure for working out energy efficiency*

The main objective breaks down into two separate tasks, first to collect data, then to submit it to a special program that makes the calculation. The first task is what is going to interest our surveyors. When you break that down you find six main tasks, which would become the highest levels of your web site.

Now look at what happens when we break down the first sub-task, classifying structural details:

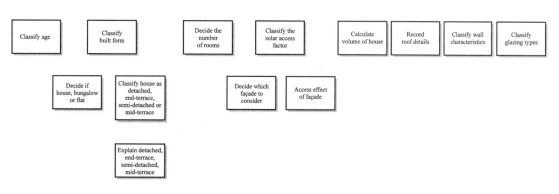

*Figure 5.7: Detailed procedure for classifying structural details*

You are now starting to get down to the basic levels of performance. At this level you can start to see what individual pages you will need. To plan your pages, draw a circle around groups of Post-its® that you think would make up a separate page. Consider two things when you do this:

| | |
|---|---|
| **Keep the performances separate where possible** | So, for example, it would be best to put the information on classifying age on one page, on built form on another and so on. Resist the temptation to put two performances together 'to fill up the page'. Doing that can confuse the user. |
| **Think about which pieces of information should be on the main route through the performance** | This will depend on the knowledge and skill levels of the typical user. For example, a surveyor should already be able to define the terms 'detached', 'end-terrace', etc. You would probably decide to leave that out of the main route. You could create this as a separate glossary page, and provide a hyperlink to the definition from the word on the main page. |

Establishing each sub-task as being one page is provisional at this stage. As you will see later, it is advisable to keep the amount of text and graphics on a page to about two browser windows in size. This means that the user does not have to scroll up and down through long files. When you come to write the content for each page you may find that it will take up more than this, in which case you should split the page at a suitable point.

When you have drawn circles around the Post-its®, draw lines to show the flow from page to page. Show links off to supplementary information by dotted lines.

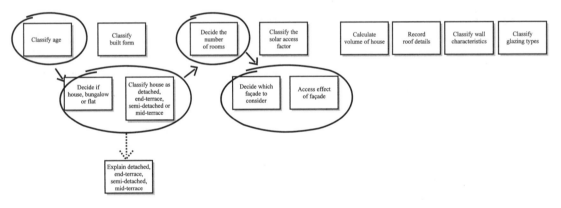

*Figure 5.8: Flow of information through classifying structural details*

This provides you with a structure on paper for your performance that you can translate readily into a web structure.

# Which method should I use?

Experience will help you decide which method may be most useful for you to follow. This table offers some ideas on how you could approach different types of material:

| | |
|---|---|
| *I need to develop a set of procedures from scratch* | 1. Establish the performance objective<br>2. Use pyramid analysis to break down the performance objective<br>3. Draft the materials from the pyramid<br>4. Think about whether to include a page or pages of FAQs on specific areas that people may find difficult |
| *I have the procedures on paper but need to structure them more clearly* | 1. Find out from the paper materials what the performance objective is<br>2. Read through the materials and use pyramid analysis to develop an outline structure<br>3. Map the paper draft on to your structure<br>4. Think about whether to include a page or pages of FAQs on specific areas that people may find difficult |
| *I have a policy document to be posted on the intranet* | 1. Ask a cross-section of users what the key words on the document are<br>2. Ask the users what questions they ask that are dealt with by the policy<br>3. Find out what information exists that corresponds to users' wants<br>4. Use this information to develop a structure bringing together your materials |
| *I want to put our monthly journal on the intranet* | 1. Write down on Post-its® a brief description of each article you want to post<br>2. Group the Post-its® as seems appropriate<br>3. Prepare a list of the general content of each group<br>4. Draw lines between articles to show which articles could be directly accessed from one another |
| *I want to put up a list of job vacancies on the intranet* | 1. Decide how to categorise the vacancies, for example by grade, location, nature of work, etc.<br>2. Write the name of each category on a Post-it®<br>3. Write an identifier for each vacancy on a Post-it®<br>4. Draw lines linking each vacancy with the category it should be linked to |

These are ideas for how to tackle specific design problems. The important thing to remember is that the methods can be mixed together, and also that the best solution is what your users want.

# Key points from the chapter

Use the method or methods that seem most appropriate. You can probably structure information that informs using the key word or FAQ method, while you will need to use pyramid analysis for instructional information.

Use people from the target group to identify key words and FAQs.

To use pyramid analysis:

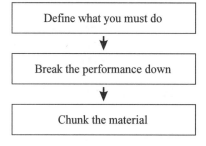

How to Design and Post Information on a Corporate Intranet

# Chapter

6

# How to write your materials

# Chapter 6
## How to write your materials

After reading this chapter you will be able to:

- prepare a set of standards that will make sure your materials are all of a consistently high quality
- write clear and effective material
- design structures for basic navigation through the information

It is only at this stage that you will start to convert your paper ideas into electronic reality. Up until now you have worked just on ideas, using paper and pens. Precision has not been important, but from now on in the project you must pay more and more attention to detail.

What are the steps you must take now?

 Make sure you know from the start what standards you are going to apply to your writing. One of the things that can really waste time is going back over text making changes to standard items. For example, it is very easy to change a method of highlighting from bold to bold italic halfway through your text by accident. Define your standards before doing anything else and you can avoid this happening.

 Decide the tone of your language. This is where having a clear picture of your target group is important. Users will only be able to understand and use your information if you have written it clearly.

 Start to write. We shall see how to use the structures you have developed in Chapter 5 to develop a plan for your writing so that you keep the content focused.

 Work out what extra text you may need to tie together the individual pages into a coherent web site.

# Define your standards

Any time that you write something you must make sure that you are consistent with spellings, punctuation, etc. If you are not, people will notice these things, and those small things will start to become all that they notice. Perception is reality, as the advertising people say, and your carefully crafted materials will be rejected as sloppy and unimportant.

This is why standards are important. You may already have a set of standards for paper-based materials, and some of these will still be valid. However, as writing for the screen needs a different style and HTML offers different possibilities, you will need to review your standards and see if you need to change anything.

If you do not have any existing standards you have a clean sheet for your intranet standards.

The table below offers some guidelines for screen-based text standards. It points out the areas where you may need to adapt existing paper-based standards to suit the different demands of the screen:

| Headings | HTML offers six sizes of heading. While you can mark a particular heading as 'Heading 1', you cannot force that to appear as, say, Times Roman 24pt bold. The browser user chooses that. What you must do is to define a standard that, say: <br><br> • the top heading on the page is Heading 1 <br> • the next most important heading is Heading 2 <br> • and so on <br><br> Make sure that the size of the heading reflects the importance of the heading. It would be dangerous to make a sub-heading larger than the main heading – while this might be an effective technique on paper, it may not work on screen. <br><br> See Chapter 7 for more information on using headings. |
|---|---|
| Capitals | Agree a policy for what words you must capitalise and which must be lower case. <br><br> Words that often cause problems are those that you may use in slightly different contexts. For example, 'manager' may need a capital M when referring to specific job title, but if you are talking about managers in general it may not. |
| References to other documents and publications | Are you going to use italics for this or put the titles within quotation marks? <br><br> Be aware that italic characters are not as clear on screen as on paper, because of the shape of screen pixels. You may therefore decide that quotation marks are more suitable. |

| | |
|---|---|
| **Use of quotation marks** | Where do you use single and double? You may opt to use double quotations for direct speech and single quotations for pointing out a word that is being used in an unfamiliar way. However, you may decide that this looks a little messy and use just one or the other for all cases. |
| **Italics** | You can italicise text with HTML but, as mentioned above, the shape of screen pixels means that the characters may not look very clear. I would therefore suggest not using italics at all. |
| **Bold** | HTML allows you to make bold characters. This is a useful technique for emphasis as they do not suffer from the same problems as italics. |
| **Emphasis** | There are a number of ways in which you can emphasise text on screen: |

**Emphasis** (continued):

*Bold* — A good choice.

*Italic* — Not a good choice, for the reasons given.

*Different colour* — This is a possibility, although it can be difficult to decide what colour to use. You need to take into consideration:

- how the colour fits in with the rest of your colour scheme
- what effect there would be if the user has set their browser to show different colours on their browser

Chapter 7 looks at using colour in more detail.

*Blinking* — You can set text to blink on and off. First-time designers of screen-based delivery are often drawn to this novelty, but it can actually be very irritating to the user. They will find that their eyes are continually drawn to the blinking text and cannot see anything else on the screen.

*Capitalisation* — When you write something by hand that you want someone to take particular notice of you may well write it in capitals. You will probably be doing this because you think that your normal handwriting is not clear enough, and this may be true!

However, in print you should never use capitals for emphasis. This is because our eyes recognise words by their shapes, not by reading each letter and cross-checking it against a mental dictionary. All completely capitalised words are essentially rectangular so they are harder to read. Using lower-case gives a word its shape, so we can read and understand it more quickly.

| **Bullet points** | Screen-based writing calls for a greater use of this technique, so you will need to define standards for this. HTML allows you to create bulleted lists and then lists within lists. (In case you come across the term, HTML refers to bulleted lists as 'unordered' lists).

However, you will have to make sure that your standards fit in with what HTML allows you to do, as it is rather prescriptive in the way it lays out bulleted lists. Also different browsers interpret the HTML bullet commands slightly differently. Look at these two interpretations of the same page. |

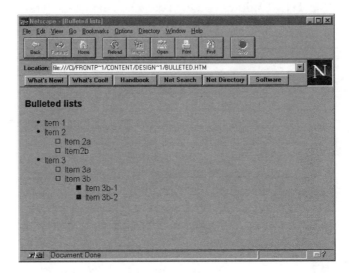

*Figure 6.1: Bulleted lists in Netscape 3*

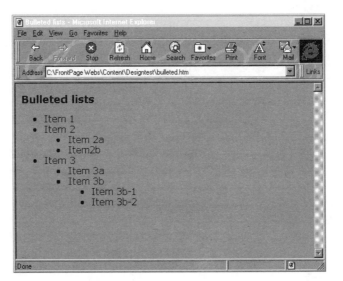

*Figure 6.2: Bulleted lists in Internet Explorer 3*

See how Netscape uses different symbols for each level of bullet while Internet Explorer uses the same for each.

Although there are restrictions on what you can do with 'straight' HTML, there are some ways around this by using tables. You can create a two column table and insert a graphic file or suitable character in the first column and the text for the bullet in the second column. We shall look at how to use tables to do this in Chapter 7.

Given these restrictions and the various ways around them, your bullet standards will need to cover:

• Are the standard HTML bullets and the paragraph formatting acceptable?

• If not, what standard approach will you follow for bulleted lists?

• How are you going to punctuate items in the list? There are various conventions in use, depending on whether the items are stand-alone sentences or continue the meaning of a stem. For example:

   • This is a complete sentence.
   • This is also a sentence.
   • Each of these must have a full stop.

However, you might have:

   • a list
   • examples
   • something else

This list uses no punctuation. Alternatively you could write it using semi-colons and a full stop, as in:

   • a list;
   • examples;
   • something else.

Whichever way you choose, be consistent. Inconsistent punctuation distracts readers from the content.

| Numbered lists | HTML calls these 'ordered' lists, and you can create these in the same way as you can unordered lists. They have the same restrictions about paragraph alignment, although you do not have the same problem with inconsistent symbols in the different browsers. |

| **Definition lists** | These are a special feature within HTML. They are a listing format designed to help you prepare such things as glossaries. This is an example: |

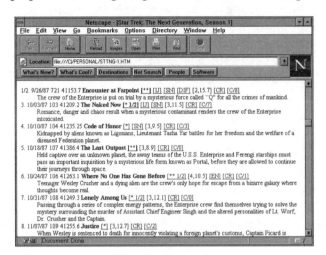

*Figure 6.3: A definition list*

Note how the format is for a heading and an indented paragraph. You can decide whether to highlight the heading in some way.

---

This list covers most of the areas for which you will need to have standards within your site. You should set these before you make a start, but do not see them as set for all time. As your experience grows and you collect feedback from users, change standards as necessary. But do not change your standards within one document or site!

# 2 Decide on the tone to use

Before you start to write your materials you need to decide the tone you are going to use. This depends on two things:

- what the users like reading

- what the material is

| Write for your readers | In Chapter 4 you saw how to build up a picture of your users. This will have given you an idea about whether they respond best to a serious or light-hearted tone, whether they like the personal style of 'You do this ...' or whether they would prefer a more impersonal style. You will have a good idea about their reading abilities, so that you know whether they would understand a more complex style of writing. It can be very difficult to write for a mixed audience and escape criticism that it is patronising some people while taxing others. Only by keeping a picture of the users in your head as you write can you produce something that satisfies most people. |
|---|---|
| Think about the content | You must also take the nature of the material into account. Consider the difference between documents describing how to make a travel expense claim, the results of the summer squash league and details of a redundancy programme. You do not need anyone to tell you that you should write the last two with a very different tone. |

## General guidelines for writing

There is not enough space in this book to go into great detail about how to write well. What I will do here is give you some basic ideas for how you can make your writing clearer for your users. If you want to explore the subject further, there is an excellent book dedicated to the subject called *The Plain English Guide* by Martin Cutts and published by Oxford University Press, 1995. I have, with permission of Oxford University Press, drawn some of these guidelines from this book.

### 1. Write in clear, easy to understand language

What it is always important to remember is that any material written with performance in mind should be *as clear as possible*. Here, English can be our best friend or our worst enemy. It is a very rich language, made so by the waves of people that have invaded and occupied the islands over the centuries. The Normans, in particular, brought their French, and this soon became the language of scholarship and government. As French merged with Anglo-Saxon, we acquired a two-tier language. Educated people learned a more sophisticated, complex and polysyllabic vocabulary, while those who did not made do with good old simple, monosyllabic Anglo-Saxon. And this persists until today. Schools teach us to use clever words like 'obtain' and to avoid the crude 'get'. Unfortunately these more sophisticated words tend to be harder to use, as they often have more complicated grammatical rules associated with them (for example, do you say 'different to' or different from'?).

Sometimes such words are only exactly correct in very specific contexts, which is why people learning the language can sound awkward.

For this reason, when writing English for instructional or informational purposes, use simple language where possible. For example, think about your own writing and see whether you can in future make the following substitutions:

| Official language | Plain language |
|---|---|
| advise | tell, inform |
| alleviate | ease, reduce |
| as a consequence of | because |
| calculate | work out |
| concerning | about |
| defer | put off |
| despite the fact that | although, despite |
| discontinue | stop, end |
| expenditure | spending |
| facilitate | help |
| hitherto | until now |
| in conjunction with | with |
| in lieu of | instead of |
| nevertheless | even so |
| necessitate | need, have to |
| reimburse | repay |
| stipulate | lay down, state |
| terminate | end, stop |
| whereby | because of which |
| with regard to | about, concerning |

(Acknowledgements to Martin Cutts, *The Plain English Guide*)

## 2. Make it personal

When users are reading through your material, they will be interested in how it affects them – 'What do *I* do next?' For that reason, use 'you' in your writing.

## 3. Keep sentences short

Long sentences are hard to follow. As we read on through a sentence, the start disappears into the dim and distant past. Then after so long we forget it completely and have to go back and read it again. Aim to keep your *average* sentence length to between 15 and 20 words. Do not try to make every sentence this length; your writing will start to lose any sense of rhythm and will sound staccato. Mix short sentences (which you can use to give key messages extra effect) with longer ones.

> If you do write a sentence that you think is too long, you can:
>
> - split and disconnect it – split it into two sentences at a suitable point
>
> - split and connect it – use a comma and a word like 'but' or 'also'
>
> - cut out repetition – look at each word and decide whether it is really necessary
>
> - make a list – split the sentence into a bulleted or numbered list
>
> - start again

Bulleted lists are an important tool on an intranet. HTML makes it easy to write such lists, so always consider them as an option where you need to break up a sentence.

## 4. Keep paragraphs short

Long paragraphs give a screen a very dense look, which can be very discouraging to a reader. To quote H W Fowler:

> The purpose of paragraphs is to give the reader a rest. The writer is saying to him: 'Have you got that? If so, I'll go on to the next point.'
>
> ... A reader will address himself more readily to his task if he sees from the start that he will have breathing spaces from time to time than if what is before him looks like a marathon course.
> (H W Fowler, *Fowler's Modern English Usage*, 2nd Edition, Oxford University Press)

Fowler may have been writing in 1926, but his advice is as relevant now as it was then. Use your eye and common sense to decide on paragraph breaks, but, as a rule of thumb, if you find that a paragraph is more than eight lines long, try to break it up.

## 5. Use the active voice

Information written using the active, rather than the passive, voice is easier to understand. The sort of material you will be putting on the intranet will often be telling people how to do something. For example, 'Write your name in the box' tells you exactly what to do, whereas 'Your name is written in the box' could mean the same, or that it has already been written, or that someone else will write it in later. If used carelessly, passive sentences can be ambiguous.

The passive voice is useful in certain circumstances, and the extent to which you can use it depends on the reading abilities of your target group. However, when writing information-oriented material make sure that less than 20% of your sentences contain passives even for sophisticated readers. Make sure that where you do use the passive voice you do not introduce any ambiguities.

### 6. Use active headings

Avoid long sequences of paragraphs one after the other. Use headings to break up the text and show what is in the paragraphs. For example, notice how the headings in this section summarise what the sections contain. 'Use the active voice' says more than 'Active and passive voices'.

### 7. Avoid using negatives

You may have heard a story about the person who found a five-year old child pointing a shotgun at him. He said 'Don't pull the trigger!', and of course the boy pulled the trigger. True or not, it shows how powerful words like 'pull' stick more easily in our minds than weak words like 'don't'. The lesson for us is to tell people what to do, rather than what not to do.

Somewhere to be particularly careful about using negatives is in lists of instructions. For example:

---

Conditions for using an official car:

You must
- have your line manager's approval
- not use it for private purposes
- complete Form PT312A

---

Note there are two positives and one negative command. This is confusing, and would be better rewritten as:

---

Conditions for using an official car:

You must
- have your line manager's approval
- complete Form PT312A

You must not use it for private purposes.

---

### 8. Keep it concise

Keep information as short as possible. Avoid adding extra text that does not help the user do what they want to do. Remember that with hyperlinking you can add extra information that is off the main track, but do this sparingly if it is not essential.

Keep in mind who you are writing for. Newcomers to a subject will need more complete information put in front of them, whereas experts would possibly prefer definitions and other background information available in a glossary accessed through a hyperlink.

Users may not be working through pages sequentially, so avoid making references in relative terms to other information. Avoid phrases like 'Earlier in this section we saw ...', say instead 'This subject is covered under 'Classifying structural details: windows' '.

Pyramid analysis is a good technique to use when you want to keep your material concise. Once you have developed your pyramid you can rewrite the text on each Post-it® and you have your information. You can see how to do this later in this chapter.

How to Design and Post Information on a Corporate Intranet

### 9. Make your point first, then expand

If you look at the structure of newspaper articles you will see that the first paragraph puts across the most important points, then the rest of the article expands on these. Use the same technique for web page writing. Your user will only see the top of the page when it first loads, so you must make sure that what they see at the top of the page captures their interest and makes them want to see what else there is on the page.

You can adapt this technique and use it throughout a page. Compare the two ways in which this passage is presented.

Method 1:

```
You enjoy being close and intimate with friends and value their
affection towards you.  However, you can maintain your own sense
of self-sufficiency and confidence about who you are.  Fulfilment
does not mean that you are dependent other people for your
happiness.  If their going away would destroy your life beyond
repair, you could not say that you were fulfilled when being with
them.

You are positive about what you and others do.  You encourage
other people both directly through what you say, and also just by
being there for them.
```

Method 2:

| | |
|---|---|
| **Be close and intimate but retain your identity** | You enjoy being close and intimate with friends and value their affection towards you.  However, you can maintain your own sense of self-sufficiency and confidence about who you are.  Fulfilment does not mean that you are dependent other people for your happiness.  If their going away would destroy your life beyond repair, you could not say that you were fulfilled when being with them. |
| **Be positive about yourself and others** | You are positive about what you and others do.  You encourage other people both directly through what you say, and also just by being there for them. |

You probably found Method 2 much easier to read and understand. Notice how the left-hand column:

* summarises the key points in the right-hand column

* catches your eye and provides a quick introduction to the content

Techniques such as this are very effective when you are presenting information.

These are useful guidelines to follow when writing any sort of text for instructional or information purposes. We can next see how to take our outline structure and write appropriate text using these guidelines.

There are various software tools available that can help you check your style, such as the grammar checker built into Microsoft® Word 6™, which I have used to write this book. They are particularly useful for spotting passive sentences and calculating measures of reading difficulty. However, checking grammar is an extremely complex task for a computer, and such tools are not perfect and can make incorrect and irritating suggestions. In spite of this I think that they are valuable to use as a first line of testing. After all, it is easier to deal with a computer criticising your English writing ability than a colleague!

# Write your content

You will find it easiest if you break down your writing into four separate stages:

| | |
|---|---|
| **1. Write the raw text** | Write everything out as you would if you were delivering it on paper (but remember the differences in writing style). |
| **2. Break it into chunks** | Decide how to break the text up, by thinking about the balance between one idea per page and practical page lengths. |
| **3. Ask a colleague to check it** | Ask someone to give you constructive criticism. |
| **4. Work out where the hyperlinks go** | Decide how to link the separate pages together. |

## 1. Write the raw text

So far we have not used a computer at all. Now is the time to switch it on and start writing. At this point you may wonder whether to use a word processor or your HTML editor. To some extent it depends on how you are going to add the HTML code.

If you are going to add the coding manually, you will need to have the text available in a plain ASCII file. If this is the case, the best thing to do is first to use a word processor that you know well. Word processors are designed for writing text, and offer better support in terms of spelling and grammar checkers, for example. Write all your text in the word processor, then save it as an ASCII text file. You can then use a text editor such as Notepad to add the HTML.

If you are going to use a package such as FrontPage, you could type everything straight into that. While it does have a spell checker, it does not check grammar. You will also be creating lots of different files that will take more time to create and make first level checking with colleagues harder than if you were working on a single file. The best way is again to use a word processor, then paste text in to the editor from the main file as required. However, note that you should be very careful about adding special character formatting in the word processor, as your HTML editor may not accept it. The safest thing to do is simply to save everything as plain ASCII text. But experiment, and see what your chosen editor will accept.

## 2. Break it into chunks

Once you have written your first draft text, you must decide how to break it into chunks. These will then become individual pages. The overall idea with chunking is to make sure that you are presenting *one idea per page*. To a large extent you will already have done that if you have worked through one of the methods for structuring described in Chapter 5.

If you have used:

| keywords | Use each of the keywords to produce a chunk. |
| --- | --- |
| FAQs | Provide the answer to each question as a separate chunk. |
| pyramid analysis | Make each substantial performance a separate chunk. |

These are useful as starting points. However, you may need to refine your chunking to take various factors into account. For example:

| Do not make the page too long | If pages contain too much material the user has to scroll up and down too much. This makes it harder to follow everything on the page.<br><br>Some scrolling is acceptable: as a rule of thumb, aim for a maximum length of twice the screen height. If it is longer than that, split into 'sub-chunks', for example, Chunk 1 into Chunks 1a and 1b. |
| --- | --- |
| Do not make the page too short | Conversely, if the page is too short, the user will be quickly clicking on the button to load the next page. This takes time and may become frustrating if they keep having to do it.<br><br>Therefore if the page length is less than a screenful, and there is a logical link between it and the next page in the sequence, try to join them together as one page. |
| Keep the file size less than 32kb | Text on its own takes up little disk space, but when you start adding graphic files, the size rises quickly. This has implications for how quickly a page loads in to the browser, so keep an eye on how big the file is.<br><br>If it grows to bigger than 32kb, see if you can break the page up to give you smaller files. |
| Provide a single large file for people to print or save | If you think users may want to save a copy of the files to their local hard disk for future use, or if they want to print it off, you can provide them with one single file.<br><br>But provide this as an alternative: the default should be separate files. Give them the option somewhere at the top of the structure to use the single large file. |
| Think about future page maintenance | If you think the site is going to need regular maintenance, remember that it is much easier to work on separate small files than one large one. |

How to Design and Post Information on a Corporate Intranet

| Decide whether to include supporting information separately or in the main text | In some cases you may not be sure whether you should write something as supplementary material, or whether to incorporate it into the main logical flow. Look at how substantial the material would be if it were standing on its own. Does it make sense? If it does, make it supplementary. If not, put it in the flow. |
| --- | --- |

## 3. Ask a colleague to check it

Once you have written your first draft, you should give it to a colleague for them to check it through and point out any typos, non-standard spellings, etc. When they are happy with it, discuss it with your high performers and subject matter experts to get their approval. *It is much easier to edit the content at this stage than after you have added the HTML code and hyperlinks.*

## 4. Work out where the hyperlinks go

When you have agreed the content of the first draft, you can start to think in more detail about how to incorporate hyperlinks. You may already have an overall idea about which pages link together, but now you need to confirm that and work out where in the text of each page you will provide the hyperlink. Also, as you write you may find that other useful links become apparent.

Hyperlinks are arguably the most powerful feature about intranet delivery, but you must treat them with care. Here are some working guidelines:

| Use hyperlinks for a good reason | Hyperlinks in a passage of text draw the user's eye and affect their reading of the passage. Also, when a user sees a hyperlink they will probably think they ought to go and look at it just to make sure they are not missing anything.

Unnecessary hyperlinks can therefore interrupt the user's flow through the material and make your material less effective. |
| --- | --- |

| | |
|---|---|
| **Write normally and do not give instructions** | So far you have written the text without giving any thought to special instructions for the hyperlinks. This is because people very quickly get used to the idea that underlined text can lead them somewhere else if they click on it. You do not have to tell them to click on the text.

Look at these two examples:

**Example 1:**

**How to remove a wheel**

```
Remove the hub cap and put it face down on the
ground.
Slacken the wheel nuts so that they are just loose
enough to be removed with your fingers.
Jack the car up so that the wheel to be changed is
off the ground.
Remove the wheel nuts and put them inside the hub
cap.
Remove the wheel.
```

<u>Click here to see how to jack the car up.</u>

**Example 2:**

**How to remove a wheel**

```
Remove the hub cap and put it face down on the
ground.
Slacken the wheel nuts so that they are just loose
enough to be removed with your fingers.
```
<u>Jack the car up</u> ``so that the wheel to be changed is
off the ground.
Remove the wheel nuts and put them inside the hub
cap.
Remove the wheel.``

Anyone with more than five minutes' experience of the Internet or an intranet will know that underlined text means that there is a hyperlink. It is not therefore necessary to add words like 'Click here to ...' Just incorporate the hyperlink message within your text as in Example 2, but make sure that it is clear where this link will take the user.

A particular fault to avoid is something like:

<u>Click here</u> `to see how to jack the car up.`

This breaks the guideline above, and also makes life hard for visually impaired users relying on screen reading software that is picking up the hyperlinks. It would just tell the user: 'Click here'. Why should they? |

| | |
|---|---|
| **Keep your hyperlinked text short** | Keep the amount of text you underline as short as you can, but make sure it is clear what it refers to. It is confusing for users if they have to read a long line of hyperlinked text, especially if it extends over two or more lines. |
| **Highlight differences in lists** | If you are offering the user a list to choose from, highlight the differences in the list, not the similarities. For example:<br><br>`How to classify the `<u>`age`</u><br>`How to classify the `<u>`built form`</u><br>`How to count the `<u>`number of rooms`</u><br>`How to classify the `<u>`solar access factor`</u><br>`How to calculate the `<u>`house volume`</u><br><br>You do not need to include the 'How to ...' statements as part of the hyperlink. |
| **Identify links within pages** | Most hyperlinks will take the user to another page. However, you can set up a hyperlink that takes the user to another point within the same page. If you do this, tell the user that this is going to happen. People expect to see a new page, and can get confused if they realise that the hyperlink has just taken them to somewhere lower down the same page. |
| **Make the hyperlinks flow** | Hyperlinks are one of the first things your users will read. They will probably scan through each one from top to bottom before reading the main text.<br><br>They will be more comfortable doing this if there is some sort of sequence to the hyperlinks. |

# What is a good way to plan hyperlinks?

Keeping these guidelines in mind, decide where your hyperlinks are going to go. You may find the following method useful for planning.

You will need:
- printouts of your text, with each planned page on a separate sheet (cut the paper to the size of the text, as this will save space)
- a pin board or similar surface
- cotton or string
- map pins

1. Fix the first two pages in your sequence to the pin board.

2. Use the map pins and cotton to connect the hyperlinking text on the first page to the second page.

3. Add the other pages one at a time, showing the hyperlinks to each. Do not bother showing hyperlinks back to a home page or to other parts of the intranet.

The case studies for two of the scenarios show how this works.

This may seem a rather elaborate way of doing it, but you will find that the network of linkages even in a small web start to become very confusing. Having a wall covered with highly visible physical linkages will be a big help in keeping track of things.

If you copy the structure of this on to paper you will have a useful permanent record of the two-dimensional structure of the web. This will be very useful when you start to test the programming of the hyperlinks later in the process.

At this point, let us look at how we would deal with our case studies.

Our session with users in Chapter 5 gave us some outline ideas for what we could write to help people with the idea of fulfilment. You can do some research into these areas and start to put together some ideas.

Page 1:

### How do people feel when they are fulfilled?

It is hard to come up with an exact list of how you might feel if you were fulfilled. However, you might notice some of the following.

| | |
|---|---|
| **Be close and intimate but retain your identity** | You enjoy being close and intimate with friends and value their affection towards you. However, you can maintain your own sense of self-sufficiency and confidence about who you are. Fulfilment does not mean that you are dependent other people for your happiness. If their going away would destroy your life beyond repair, you could not say that you were fulfilled when being with them. |
| **Be positive about yourself and others** | You are positive about what you and others do. You encourage other people both directly through what you say, and also just by being there for them. |
| **Are you self-actualised?** | Fulfilled people can be described as 'self-actualised'. This is a term associated with Abraham Maslow, who put forward an idea that people have to satisfy a 'hierarchy of needs'. Self-actualisation is the last of these needs, and to satisfy it you have to achieve the others. People who have achieved it show the feelings described above. They are happy with their own company and are accepting of themselves and others. |

Page 2:

### What can you do to work towards a sense of fulfilment?

A sense of fulfilment is not something that you can obtain overnight. You will have to work at it, and it may mean having to make changes in your lifestyle if you come to realise that that is what is actually a problem.

Maslow's hierarchy of needs puts forward the idea that to become fulfilled (or 'self-actualised' as it says in his theory) you have to satisfy other, lower-level needs:

**physiological**         basic bodily needs such as food and drink

**security**              protection from danger

**social**                love, friendship and being with people whose company you enjoy

**self-esteem**           self-respect and autonomy

**self-actualisation**    fulfilment through realising your potential

By taking steps to make sure that you satisfy each lower-level need in turn you can move up the hierarchy until you reach self-actualisation.

That sounds simple enough, but what are the steps you can take to make that happen?

**Set yourself goals you can achieve.**

Every week think about what you want to have achieved by the end of the week. These might be personal, to have invited your next-door neighbours around for coffee or to have telephoned a long-lost friend; or to do with work, to have finished writing a report. At the end of the week check to see if you have achieved them.

**Make goals achievable but stretching**
You will not reach fulfilment by achieving goals that you would have achieved anyway.

**Clarify what is important to you**
What do you really want? Do you want to have lots of money or do you want to be professionally or personally successful? You may not be able to achieve all of these, and to feel fulfilled you will need to decide what is the right balance for you.

**Live life directly**
Nobody ever achieved fulfilment through watching television or playing computer games. You will need to get out and engage with life. Meet people, talk to them, strike up conversations with strangers. You could make one of your goals to talk to someone you don't know at the bus stop.

**Read more and try something out**
There are many books that you could look through. There are also courses available at the Training and Development Centre that may help.

Page 3:

**What is there that I can read or do next?**

There are some training courses available at the Training and Development Centre that will help.  The Training Prospectus explains what there is.

Achieving fulfilment is something that alternative bookshops often have information about.  They will stock interesting books and have details about local courses and workshops.  Here are some books that you may find helpful:

M Scott Peck, *The Road Less Travelled*, Rider, 1978

J Canfield & M V Hansen, *Chicken Soup for the Soul*, Health Communications Inc., 1993

R Skynner & J Cleese, *Life and How to Survive it*, Methuen, 1993

After writing this draft, think about how to split up the pages.  Each of the three sections looks substantial enough to be in its own, so you could split it up as shown.  When you come to lay out the pages, Page 2 may seem too long, but you can sort that out later.

How does the writing style follow the guidelines?

- There is one main idea on each page.

- Just 10% of the sentences are in the passive voice.

- The average sentence length is 17.6 words.

- The grammar checker on Word 6 tells you that its Flesch Reading Ease is 69.3 (on a 0 to 100 scale, where 100 is the easiest).  The score for standard writing is between 60 and 70, so this means that our text is suitable for the target group.

- The headings are worded actively.

- Key messages are brought out to be more visible.

The next step is to work out how to link the pages together.  Our string and pin board could look like this:

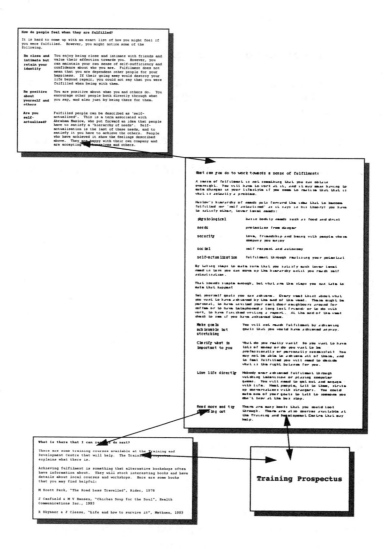

*Figure 6.4: The pin board exercise for the fulfilment section*

When you do this, you will start to realise how you may need to reword certain phrases so that you can add meaningful hyperlinks.

You may also start to see where hyperlinks from within each page might come. For example, you might think it would be useful to link 'hierarchy of needs' on Page 1 with the section on this subject on Page 2. This however, would just duplicate a linear link from Page 1 to Page 2 and would confuse users. It would be valid if the section on Maslow were on a separate page. Having this visual display of the text makes such possibilities seem clearer. If you think it would be good to separate it (and Page 2 is possibly too long), try it.

How to Design and Post Information on a Corporate Intranet

**Scenario 2**
Customer: *'I think the intranet would be a better way of delivering this information on safe manual handling procedures. Can you do that for me?'*

Before you start writing, look at the pyramid we developed for this performance:

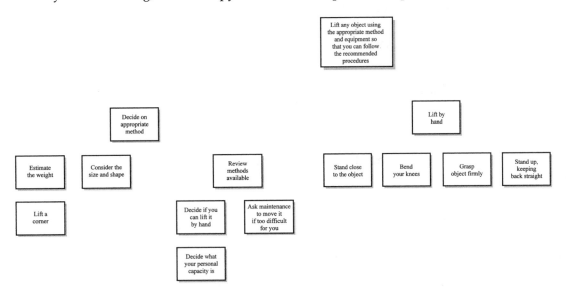

*Figure 6.5: Pyramid analysis for a safe manual load handling procedure*

Use what is written here as a basis for your text:

```
Page 1: Decide how to lift the object
```

```
Before you lift anything, decide what is the best way to do it.
```

```
Estimate the weight     You can do this by trying to lift a corner.
```

```
Think about its         Large, light objects can be as difficult to carry
size and shape          as small, heavy ones.
```

```
Decide if you can       If you have any doubts, think about finding another
lift it safely          way of doing it.  Call someone from maintenance to
                        help.
```

```
If you think you can lift it yourself, make sure you do it the right way.
```

```
Page 2: How to lift the object safely
```

```
If you decide you can lift it by hand, then:
```

```
Stand close to the object.
```

```
Get down to the object by bending your knees.  Keep your back straight.
```

```
Grasp the object firmly.
```

```
Stand up, keeping your back straight.
```

See how this follows our guidelines:

- There is one main idea on each page.

- The two pages will both be of a reasonable length, bearing in mind that we will probably add some graphics to illustrate the text, and we will also have general navigational features to incorporate.

- Everything is written in the active voice.

- The average sentence length is 9.8 words.

- The Flesch Reading Ease is 90.5, very simple. This makes it suitable for the target group, which will include people with limited reading skills.

- The two headings are worded actively.

You must next work out where to add hyperlinks. As the first page simply links to the second, there will only be one. The best thing to do would be:

```
If you are sure you can lift it yourself, make sure you do it
the right way.
```

This hyperlink will tell the user that this will take them to a page that will show them how to lift the right way.

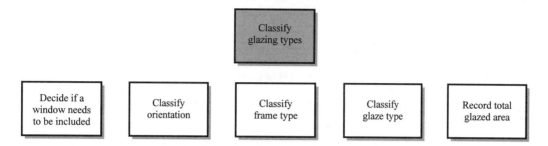

**Scenario 3**
Customer: *'We need some on-line guidance for our field surveyors on how to work out the energy efficiency of domestic properties. We haven't got anything at the moment.'*

Start off by looking at the pyramids. We shall look at the section on classifying glazing types.

| | | Classify glazing types | | |
|---|---|---|---|---|
| Decide if a window needs to be included | Classify orientation | Classify frame type | Classify glaze type | Record total glazed area |

*Figure 6.6: Procedure for classifying glazing types*

You can now start writing:

**Do I include every window?**

Windows have two possible effects on energy efficiency. They can lose energy through the glass but also let light pass through to warm up that room. This is known as **solar gain**. For this reason you may need to count a glazed door as a window for energy rating purposes.

This decision tree shows how to do this:

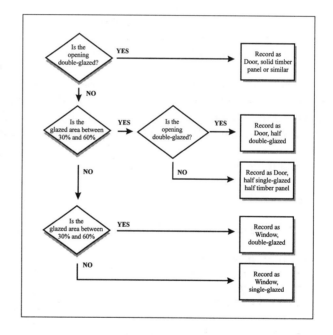

**Do sloping windows count?**

Windows in roofs and other sloping windows may be difficult to classify. Depending on their slope and orientation, you may have to count them as roof lights.

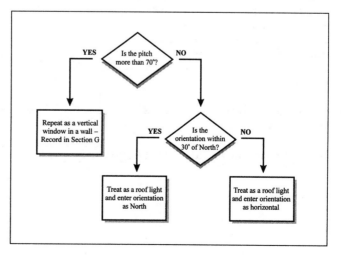

### What effect do conservatories have?

You do not need to consider the effects of a conservatory if it is separated from the property by an external-quality door. However, you should apply a shelter factor to the wall and/or windows separating the dwelling and conservatory.

If it is separated by an internal door, record the glazing details as if it were any other window. In this case, do not include details about windows facing into the conservatory.

How does this follow our guidelines?

- Most of it is written in the active voice; 21% of it is passive.

- The average sentence length is 12.1 words.

- The Flesch Reading Ease is 61.6. This reflects the percentage of passive sentences, but this is acceptable for the target group.

- The headings are worded actively.

You would probably split the page into two, starting the second at the section on sloping windows. It would probably be too long as one page, and we need to avoid having a very short page, such as one with two paragraphs about conservatories.

You would also be aware that the decision tree about sloping windows is relevant to a section on roofs. You might therefore decide to put that decision tree on a separate page that both sections and the one on roofs can link to. This would save disk space and would make maintenance of that graphic easier, should regulations change.

You would therefore amend the two pages thus:

**Page 1:**

### Do I include every window?

Windows have two possible effects on energy efficiency. They can lose energy through the glass but also let light pass through to warm up that room. This is known as **solar gain.** For this reason you may need to count a glazed door as a window for energy rating purposes.

This decision tree shows how to do this.

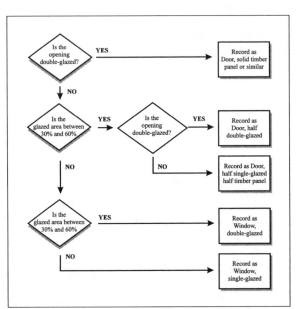

Sloping windows and conservatories

**Page 2:**

### Do sloping windows count?

Windows in roofs and other sloping windows may be difficult to classify.  Depending on their slope and orientation, you may have to count them as <u>roof lights</u>.

### What effect do conservatories have?

You do not need to consider the effects of a conservatory if it is separated from the property by an external-quality door. However, you should apply a shelter factor to the wall and/or windows separating the dwelling and conservatory.

If it is separated by an internal door, record the glazing details as if it were any other window.  In this case, do not include details about windows facing into the conservatory.

When you have decided which windows you must include, you need to classify their <u>orientation</u>.

You can now get your pin board out and start to plot the hyperlinks.  It would start out looking something like this:

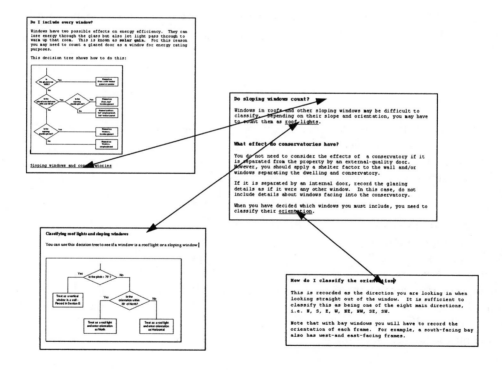

*Figure 6.7:  The pin board exercise for the section on windows*

This part of the chapter has shown you how to work out the detailed linkages between different pages.  You will now need to work out what the overall structure of the site should be.

# 4

# Set up the way through the material for the users

When you know exactly how you are going to break up your text, you can start to plan how a user can navigate through it. There are several ways in which web sites can be structured.

### 1. Hierarchical

Multiple options on each page lead to a pyramid of pages.

The overall structure of sites usually resembles this, as it is a very easy way to organise information.

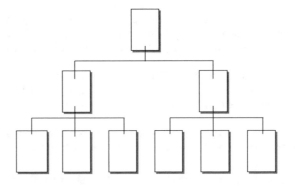

### 2. Linear

The user moves from one page to the next. This works well for procedural information.

### 3. Web

This may be the type of structure we think of when we use the word 'web site'. It is not necessarily a very practical way of organising information.

Sites with collections of loosely related pieces of information may resemble it, but users can find it confusing to use. It may be acceptable for esoteric information sources on the World Wide Web, but it does lend itself to delivering effective organisational information.

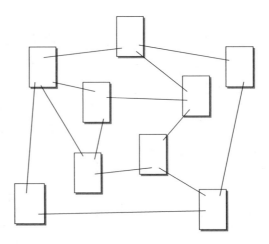

In reality most intranet sites use a mixture of the first two techniques. At the macro level information is classified in a hierarchical way, then at the micro level the linear approach is used.

How to Design and Post Information on a Corporate Intranet

The typical site will be structured something like this:

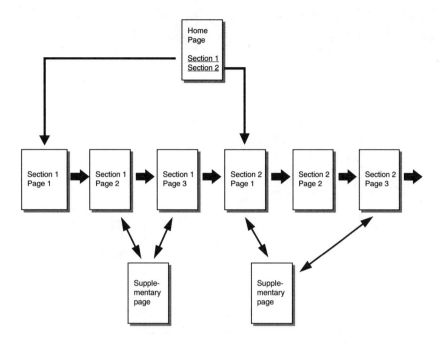

*Figure 6.8 A typical web site structure*

In web jargon, the first page of any section is called the home page. When your intranet users open their browser, the first page they will see will probably be the intranet home page. From this they may choose to go to their department's own home page, and so on.

The user can then go from the home page to the start of each section, and from one section to the next. They will also be able to visit supplementary pages as required. What are not shown here are the other links necessary on each page; every page must have basic navigational controls to allow the user to move back to the home page and to other parts of the intranet. This is covered in detail in Chapter 7.

The user therefore navigates through a combination of menus, going straight on and visits to supplementary material. Each step is enabled by a hyperlink.

Your complete intranet will have its own menu structure that will allow a user to find their way down to your materials. The principles of developing a menu structure are the same at whatever level you are working, so let us look at how this could work for two of our scenarios.

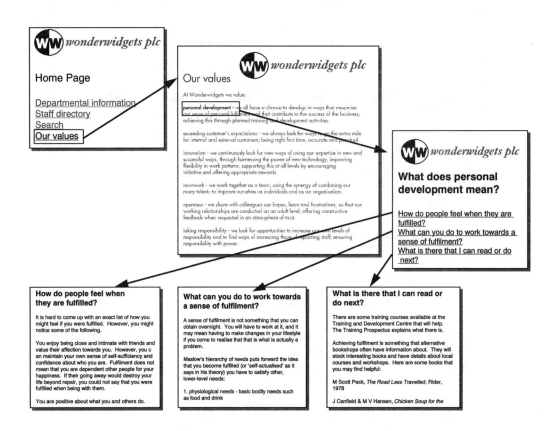

*Figure 6.9: High level structure for the Wonderwidgets intranet*

We are using FAQs to let people explore the answers to questions they may have after reading the values statement.

The menu structure to let the surveyors find their information on energy rating could work like this:

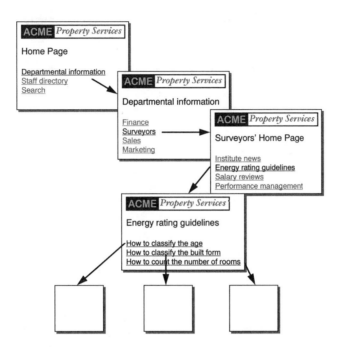

*Figure 6.10: High level structure for the ACME Property Services intranet*

Notice how surveyors can find the information they need on this subject at the fourth level. It is important to keep the hierarchy of menus as thin as possible. If users have to work through more than four levels of information to find the specific information they need, they will start to become disoriented and will lose interest.

You have seen in this chapter how to write the raw text. In Chapter 7 you will see how to take this text and integrate it with graphics to produce finished pages.

# Key points from the chapter

- Define your standards before you start writing.

- Make the tone you use appropriate for the readers and the content.

- Write clearly, avoiding long sentences.

- Break the text up into page-sized chunks, each of which represents one major idea.

- Plan where to put the hyperlinks.

# Chapter 7

# How to design your pages

# Chapter 7
## How to design your pages

After reading this chapter you will be able to:

- prepare a specification for the look of your intranet pages

- list all the control features needed

There are two steps to designing your pages:

**Decide which tools to use**

Decide how you are going to add the HTML code.  Are you going to do it manually using raw HTML, or are you going to use a web authoring package that does most of the work for you?  Chapter 1 discusses some of the leading packages available.

Then you need to work out your overall page design.  This is about using an appropriate balance of:

- background

- text

- graphics

In addition, you will need to decide whether you are going to design a framed site.

**Use the tools**

In this step you have to:

- set up navigational controls

- add editorial features

- lay out the text

Once you have written your raw text, you can start to think about how it will all look on screen.  You will do this through your HTML editor.  This chapter will show you how to produce basic screen designs using Microsoft FrontPage.  This is a true WYSIWYG editor, with a very similar feel to Word 6, so if you are used to that package you should be able to learn FrontPage quickly.  FrontPage is a complex package about which whole books have been written, and this book does not attempt to show you how to use every aspect of it.  What it will do is demonstrate how the package can be used, and how you can use FrontPage to do certain key things.

I shall not cover how to use HTML here, as there are a large number of books dedicated to just that subject and it is beyond the scope of this book. In fact, FrontPage allows you to use most of the features of basic HTML, and only if you wanted to integrate HTML pages with databases and other business software would you find it lacking.

However, it is important to realise that despite the apparent sophistication of FrontPage, it is simply a program that creates HTML files. As such it is limited by HTML, so you will find that there are some formatting techniques that you use on paper that you just cannot do on screen. There are, however, various tricks that you can employ to make your screens work in the way you want them to. I shall cover some of these here, but you will need to study some of the more specialised literature if you want to find out more about the subtleties of web page design. There are also a number of sites on the World Wide Web where you can find information. Some of these are listed in the Bibliography.

A word of caution! When desktop publishing packages first appeared, many people thought they would be able to design wonderful, attractive paper documents. They could, but only if they had the graphic design skill in the first place. Having a first-class set of tools does not mean that you will be able to use them to make something perfect. If you do not have a graphic designer's eye, do not try to use all the tricks that modern graphics and HTML authoring packages make available, as your lack of skill in that area will become painfully obvious. Concentrate instead on what you are good at, and focus on developing clean, easy to use page designs. If you really want to design something eye-catching, find a professional graphic designer to help you.

**Decide which tools to use**

Users will form an impression about the value of each page as soon as it appears in their browser window. They will decide whether it is interesting and attractive before reading any of the content. The look of the page can also say a lot about your organisational image: a dull, graphic-free site might suggest a somewhat dull and unattractive working environment, whereas screens with pleasing colours and modern graphic design would suggest an up-to-date, image-conscious organisation.

Before you do anything about colours and graphics, have a good think about what is going on your pages. What will each page typically contain? Will there be a lot of text, will there be graphics? How will the web be linked together, and what implications does this have for navigation? Start to think about how these elements could be arranged to make each page attractive and usable.

When you have a reasonable idea of what each page will contain and how it might be laid out, you can start to consider the tools that you need in order to make that happen. There are essentially three of these:

- background – the overall pattern or colour of the page
- foreground – the text
- eye-catchers – graphics and other screen elements, such as frames

I call them tools because they are of no value on their own: they only become important when you start to do something with them. In this first part of the chapter we shall look at the issues that you need to take into consideration when using the tools. In Step 2 you will see how to use them to start putting your pages together.

You will integrate the background, text and graphics to make attractive, usable pages, but you must remember that you have limited control over what actually appears on the users' screens. When you use a desktop publishing package you can design a page and know that it will come out of the printer looking exactly as you have intended. It can then be reproduced so that everyone in your organisation receives an identical copy.

However, you do not have the same degree of control over browser users. Although in theory all browsers can read HTML files equally well, there are text-only browsers that will not show any graphics. There are differences between the monitors on Apple Mac, PCs and UNIX workstations that will make the same files look different. Users will have different sizes and shapes for their browser window, with some having it set to full screen while others have a portrait-shaped window.

There are some other issues to be aware of:

| | |
|---|---|
| **HTML keeps developing** | HTML is a very rapidly developing language. As it develops, it introduces new features that you can incorporate into your designs, providing you know the appropriate HTML codes or have up-to-date authoring tools. For example, when HTML version 2 appeared, it introduced the ability to create tables. Version 3.2 introduced frames, where you can divide the window up into two or more separate windows. Browsers can only interpret those HTML commands that were actually part of the language when the browser was designed. So if you have an old browser, such as Netscape 2, you will not be able to load pages designed with frames.<br><br>If you know that a sizeable proportion of your audience has old versions of browsers, you will have to think about what HTML features you can use. |
| **Some people will not want your graphics** | If you have ever used the Internet you will know that one of the most frustrating things about it is the speed at which pages load. And pages that have a lot of graphics on them load more slowly still. For this reason browsers allow the user to decide whether they want to load the graphics files or not. For example, with Internet Explorer 3 you select View, Options, General, and remove the check in the appropriate box, while with Netscape 3 you remove the tick from Autoload images under Options.<br><br>Although pages load much more quickly over an internal network than on the Internet, many people (perhaps those with painful memories of using the Internet with a slow modem!) will choose not to load images. People with visual impairment also often do this. You must not therefore rely on graphics alone to convey important information. |
| **Users choose their own typefaces** | As we saw in Chapter 1, another option browser users have is over their screen typefaces, so your carefully designed Times Roman pages may be displayed by your users in Arial (or worse). |

We shall come back to some of these issues later, and see what ways there are of getting around them. The next thing to do is to make some decisions about the background, text and graphics.

# Choose your background

When someone 'merges into the background' we imagine that they disappear from view, which implies that we do not notice a background. That is clearly not true, as the background to a screen, like the colour of the walls in a room, sets a certain tone. It therefore needs to be chosen with some care, while at the same time remembering that it is just a background and that whatever colour or pattern it has must not dominate the foreground where your information is.

There are two ways of setting a background to your pages: you can choose a plain colour or you can use a graphic file to give you a patterned background. This works like Windows wallpaper; you create a small file with the full pattern you want, and the browser displays it over and over again throughout the window.

Here are some guidelines about what to be aware of when choosing backgrounds.

## Plain backgrounds

| | |
|---|---|
| **Plain backgrounds are more consistent between browsers** | The appearance of screens with plain backgrounds on different browsers is more consistent. Sometimes a pattern can look so different on a different browser that the text gets lost. |
| **Users can choose their own coloured backgrounds** | Users can choose their own coloured backgrounds that can override your choice. For example, you might leave the background as the normal grey, but a user could have set their background option to cyan. This would make any cyan text on your page disappear. If you really want users to all have the same background colour you can specify that your design colour overrides the browser option. |

**FrontPage help**
To do this:
- click the right mouse button anywhere on your page
- choose Page Properties
- check Custom Background Color
- Choose the colour you want

This colour will then show on this page regardless of what the user sets their browser to show.

However, you should be aware that users with a visual impairment often need to set their screen background colour to something unusual so that they can see the screen clearly. Forcing a particular colour may therefore make it harder for them to see the screen clearly. That may make you decide not to use the custom colour and instead to rely on fairly standard colour combinations.

| | |
|---|---|
| **Pale colours work best** | Pale colours tend to work best as backgrounds. One reason for this is that they allow a smoother contrast between foreground and background colours. Contrast is much more of a problem on computer screens than on paper because light is radiated from screens rather than reflected, as from paper. Black text on white page may be fine for paper, but it is hard on a computer user's eyes. Look instead for a softer contrast. A grey background gives a good contrast with most foreground colours and tends to bring out the colour well. Play with the colours available and test combinations with users until you arrive at a colour scheme that people find attractive and usable. |
| **Design for the simplest machines on your network** | Whenever you are playing with colour on a computer, remember that not all computers have the same ability to show colours. You may have a PC with a graphics card capable of showing millions of colours, but your end users may only have basic colour cards capable of showing 16 colours. Choose colours that work on the lowest common denominator machine. |

## Patterned backgrounds

| | |
|---|---|
| **Patterns convey messages** | Patterns can be used to give different messages. For example, a marbled background radiates corporate solidity. You may use different types of paper for different purposes: patterns can reproduce that on screen. |
| **Plan for the file not displaying** | Sometimes browsers do not load the background file, in which case the user will be looking at a plain screen. Think of the consequences of that, and whether it means you need to specify a custom colour. |
| **Think about your users** | Users with visual impairment may find screens with patterned backgrounds harder to read. Be aware of that when you design the patterns. |

If you want to get some ideas about different backgrounds, have a look at http://www.gingers.com/tile1.htm on the World Wide Web. This site has a selection of backgrounds you can download and use.

## Set up your text

If you are used to laying out paper documents you will know how you can change the look of a document by changing the typeface. Switching from Times Roman to Avant Garde makes a document look that bit more modern. With intranet pages you do not have that facility available, as the user can choose for themselves what typeface their browser displays. So do not spend any time worrying about typefaces, and think about what you can do with the text in terms of colour and other special effects.

## How to set headings

HTML defines six sizes of heading in addition to normal text. Look at this screen that shows the comparative sizes of text:

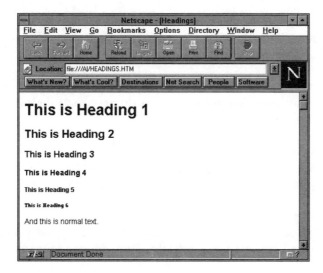

*Figure 7.1: HTML headings and normal text*

Heading 1 is the largest, going down to Heading 6, which is actually smaller than normal text. These heading sizes are fixed and you cannot change them. Before you start laying out your pages it is a good idea to think about what levels of headings you are going to need.

Use heading sizes logically. Use Heading 1 for main headings, working down to Heading 6 for the least important sub-heading. Using a smaller font for a main heading than for a sub-heading may not work very well on a web page.

## How to decide on colour

The next thing you need to consider is colour. Again, this is something your user has control over, but, as with backgrounds, you can fix the colours of text if you wish.

---

**FrontPage help**
To fix the colour:
- select the text the colour of which you want to fix
- choose Format, Characters
- check Set Color
- Choose the colour you want

This text will then appear in the colour you set on this page regardless of what the user sets their browser to show.

---

You need to consider the same issues here: that users may have set their browsers to show screen colours that are not compatible with this fixed colour.

Although you cannot control what your users see exactly, you do need to start off with a consistent combination so that, assuming that most users do have some logic in their set-ups, the pages will display clearly.

Make sure that the colours you choose for text work with the background. You will need to ensure that there is a smooth contrast between the text colours and the background. But avoid hot colours such as pink or magenta: they give too strong a contrast and can seem to throb on the screen.

Use colours for consistent reasons; do not use different colours just because your software lets you. Do not have too many colours on screen. Stick to a maximum of four colours for your text.

Remember the colour circle and the use of complementary colours. Those colours opposite each other work well together.

## Using special type styles

As with paper design, you can set text to be highlighted in various ways, such as italics, bold and underlined. You can also set text to blink on and off. Some words of warning about these methods:

- *Italics* do not work particularly well on screen, as the square pixels that make up a screen do not accommodate the sloping shape of italic characters.

- Underlining should be avoided as this is how hyperlinked text is identified. Just adding an underline does not a hyperlink make, as Shakespeare never had the opportunity to say.

- Blinking should be avoided wherever possible. Something blinking on screen makes it almost impossible to read anything else, and as such should be reserved for text that represents something going wrong, and then only as a last resort.

## Decide how to use graphics

The use of graphics on an intranet is a large and complex subject, and in this book I can only try to cover some of the key areas that you need to be aware of. The careful use of graphics is very important in making your intranet page interesting and useful. As with any delivery medium, a picture is worth a thousand words, so use graphics where they are useful.

However, you may have come across a version of this saying for the wired 1990s, that says: 'A picture is worth a thousand words, but a thousand words has a lot less bandwidth'. What is this about bandwidth? The term has nothing to do with size but with speed; it is the speed at which data can flow into your computer. The bandwidth of the Internet depends on your connection to it. For example, if you use a V34 modem, the fastest modem standard at the moment, it can send and receive data at 28,400 bits per second. A typical Ethernet network sends data at 10,000,000 bits per second (10Mbps), which is 350 times faster. Fast Ethernet networks, which are just starting to appear, work at 100Mbps.

The much smaller bandwidth of the Internet is why graphics files can take a long time to download. If you have used the Internet you will know that it can be very frustrating watching a browser receiving data for what can be several minutes with nothing happening on screen. For this reason browsers give users the option to not load graphics. If the user does select this option, the graphic file is not sent, and the browser displays a small symbol in the corner of a blank space that the graphic would occupy. There may be a line of text next to the symbol; this is known as the alternate description for the graphic, and is something that a good web designer provides for any graphic file they put on their pages.

Things are not quite so bad on an intranet as data can travel much more quickly, but the time taken to load a graphic can still be appreciable. For this reason you should use graphics with care, and remember that not everyone will want or be able to see them.

The need to minimise file size has led to the development of special techniques for encoding and transmitting graphic files.

## What types of graphic files are there?

There are two main formats for graphic files used on web-based systems. These formats have been developed to make file sizes as small as possible, and you will need to use them for any graphics you develop. However, do not think that you will have to learn any new graphics packages: most new versions of leading packages such as CorelDraw allow you to save graphics that you create in either of these two formats.

They are:

- the *GIF* format, the commonest standard. This stands for the Graphics Interchange Format, and such files have the extension .gif.

- the *JPEG* format, which stands for the Joint Photographic Experts Group. These files have the extension .jpg.

These formats work in different ways and are suitable for different types of graphic. GIF files store information on every pixel in the image, whereas JPEG allows the designer to discard information on pixels that do not affect the image too much. The result is that JPEG files can be much smaller, but GIF files are usually much sharper.

So, which to use?

| If your image has: | Use: |
| --- | --- |
| simple black and white images, straight lines | GIF |
| large areas of single colours | GIF |
| continuous colour or greyscale images, such as photographs | JPEG |

Once you have created and saved your graphic file, you can insert it in your page in the same way as you do with inline graphics in an ordinary word processor.

There are some other terms you will come across. GIFs can be:

| | |
| --- | --- |
| *animated* | A sequence of GIFs that the browser loads one after the other, quickly on top of each other. The effect is like the children's booklets with a sequence of slightly different pictures that you flick through: you get a somewhat crude animation effect. You can produce animated GIFs using special graphics packages. |
| *interlaced* | A way of making graphics appear more quickly on a browser. Imagine that a graphic is made up of 50 horizontal lines. With a normal GIF the browser waits until it has received all 50 lines before showing the graphic. With an interlaced GIF the server sends lines 1, 9, 17, etc. first, and the browser shows them as they are received. When these have all been sent, the server sends line 2, 10, 18, etc., and so on until all the file has been sent. The image therefore seems to unfurl on the screen. This is an improvement, especially for large graphic files, so if your graphics are large, say over 50kb, save them as interlaced GIFs. |
| *transparent* | These have a background through which you can see the browser background colour. You can use this technique if you want your graphics to have an irregular, rather than a rectangular, boundary. |

There are also *progressive* JPEG files. These work on a similar principle to interlaced GIFs.

A format to look out for soon may be the *Portable Network Graphic*, PNG. This can give files that are 30% smaller than in GIF format, and the files are designed to start displaying on the browser when only 1/64 of the file has been received. They also have a special feature that automatically corrects for the different technologies used in PC and Macintosh monitors. At the moment this technical difference affects the colour and contrast of graphics displayed on the two systems.

## Dithering

This is a term you may come across to describe a problem you may find with colour rendering on different types of computer. Computers can only display a certain number of colours; for many PCs this is 256, but it may be as few as 16. If your browser loads a graphic file that contains a colour not in its palette it will display a pattern of two alternate colours that it thinks represent the missing colour. This 'dithering' over the colour never looks very good and can spoil a carefully crafted graphic.

This is only really a problem with graphics containing blocks of solid colour. Photographic images usually have such a blend of colours that you would not notice the dithering.

There is a way round it. There are in fact 216 common colours that are found on all types of computer, so provided you keep to these when designing your graphics, they will never dither. You can find out what these colours are by downloading the information found at http://www.lynda.com/hex.html.

## What are the guidelines for using graphics?

The previous section provided you with some background information about how to create graphic files. In this section we shall look at some of the design issues affecting where and when to use graphics. Some of these guidelines apply to any delivery medium, while some are specific to web-based delivery.

| | |
|---|---|
| **Use graphics only when you need to** | This applies to paper-based materials as well. Using graphics for no real reason makes a page look worse, rather than better.<br><br>Use graphics to:<br>• clarify information<br>• improve the look of a page<br><br>Always try to imagine justifying your use of a graphic to someone: if you would find that difficult, leave the graphic out. |
| **Complete the alternate text tag for all graphics** | HTML allows you to attach a text description to graphic files. The browser displays this if the user has turned their graphics loading off.<br><br>**FrontPage help**<br>• Double-click on the image<br>• Type your alternate text under Alternate Representation, Text<br><br>Adding the alternate text also helps users with visual impairments relying on screen reading software. They may not be able to see a graphic, but the software will tell them what the graphic is and if it provides a hyperlink. |
| **Use graphics for hyperlinks** | You can set a graphic file to act as a hyperlink if the user clicks on it.<br><br>This can be a very effective way of setting up links that appear on every page. Instead of having a line of text that says 'Home page', you can design a small GIF file that represents the page. Repeat this for all the regular navigational features on a page.<br><br>You can also create *imagemaps*. These are graphics that have hot spots on them, special areas that can be clicked. You could for example show a floor plan of your building, showing which departments are situated where. The user could click on any area and be taken to the home page for that particular department. |

| | There are some points to take into consideration if you do use imagemaps: |
|---|---|
| | <ul><li>Some browsers do not support imagemaps, so always provide alternative text-based links.</li><li>Make the clickable areas obvious and distinct. Users do not necessarily expect that clicking on different parts of the same image does different things.</li><li>Design the clickable areas to look like buttons that they can push.</li></ul> |
| **Develop graphical themes where appropriate** | You can design graphics that relate to a consistent theme. This might be the subject of the pages or the organisation itself.<br><br>You can, for example, design graphical bullet points that categorise or highlight different items in a list. |
| **Keep an eye on the size of your graphics** | This applies to both their dimensions and their file size. You should avoid creating a web page that is over 32kb in size, so, allowing for some text, you should work towards 30kb as a maximum for any graphic file.<br><br>Also, if you think that users will want to print your pages off, keep the width to less than 535 pixels, as this is the maximum width that can be printed off on a sheet of A4 paper.<br><br>So that users will not have to scroll up and down to see all of a graphic, keep the height to less than 320 pixels. |
| **Design for your users' graphics cards** | As a web developer, you may have a 24-bit colour card that gives you over 16 million colours. However, your users may only have 8-bit cards capable of showing only 256 colours. Unless you know that every user can take advantage of 24-bit colour, design for 256 colours and keep to a maximum of about 50 colours on any single page. |
| **Store graphics on the same server as your text** | If you use the same files on many different corporate pages, it is tempting to consider saving disk space by storing all the graphic files on one server. The individual pages could then call the file off the graphics server when needed.<br><br>This is in fact not good practice. Accessing another server adds to the time taken to load the file, and there is always the chance that the server may be off-line or the files have been moved or replaced. This could cause problems for your page layout. |
| **Warn users about big graphic files on a hyperlink** | If a hyperlink leads a user to a file with a large graphic file, it is considered good practice on World Wide Web pages to warn the user, so that they can avoid the page or switch the graphics load option off. It is not so important on an intranet, but you may want to do it out of politeness! |

## Don't forget the horizontal line

HTML has an in-built horizontal line command. This generates a line that can be of any thickness and any length. You can specify it to be of a fixed number of pixels in length or it can be a percentage of the browser window width. And it can be left, right or centrally aligned.

They were included in the HTML command set as a simple way of separating text blocks visually. You can use them to:

- draw the user's attention to material that is separate to the main text, such as navigational text
- separate out text that appears periodically throughout a page length

The power of the line lies in its ability to separate: it loses that power if over-used.

---

**FrontPage help**
- Position the cursor where you want the line
- Choose Insert, Horizontal line
- Right click and choose Properties
- Change the line's properties as you wish

# Decide whether to use frames

The most recent addition to HTML's page design language is the ability to divide the screen up into frames. A framed page looks like this:

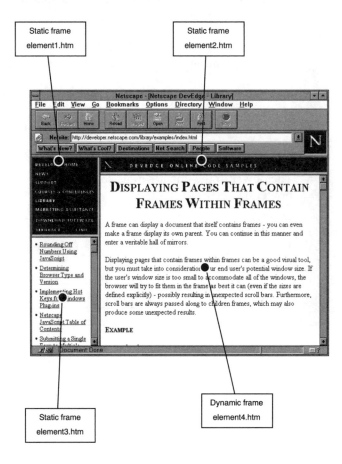

*Figure 7.2: An example of a framed site*

This is an example of a framed page developed by Netscape for its World Wide Web site. It contains four frames. What do the frames contain?

- The top left-hand frame gives hyperlinks to other parts of the Netscape site.

- The lower left-hand frame gives hyperlinks to articles that will appear in the main frame.

- The top right-hand frame simply has a graphic image as a title.

- The lower right-hand frame, the main frame, contains the text of articles.

The first three frames are referred to as 'static' frames, while the main frame is described as 'dynamic'.

How does it work? You as the user can scroll down the lower left frame to find an interesting title, then you can click on it and the text will appear in the main frame. What advantages does this offer? It means that you can separate the main navigational features of the site or page from the main text and keep them static. The user can then read the article, and at any time can click on a navigational hyperlink to move on. They will not have to scroll up or down to find the way out buttons.

Notice that the content of each of the frames is a separate HTML file. The overall page is a separate HTML file called a frameset. It contains information about which files occupy its frames and what their relationships are.

| What are the advantages? | • Frames keep a 'map' of the web site on screen at all times, helping the user to keep oriented.<br><br>• They can cut down on the level of menus that a user needs to work through. With careful design a framed site need be only one click down from the home page.<br><br>• You can provide a hyperlink to let the user go and look at another part of the intranet while keeping a presence on this part of the web. |
|---|---|
| What are the disadvantages? | • From a designer's point of view they can be more time consuming to develop.<br><br>• They are not supported by older versions of browsers. Users will need to have at least Netscape v.2 or Internet Explorer v.3. If someone with an older version tries to load a framed file, they receive a message saying that they cannot do it. Therefore, if you expect that a sizeable number of users will not be able to read framed files, you should design a non-framed version as well. Clearly this doubles your development time in duplicating information.<br><br>• You can get carried away with the possibilities! |

What are the guidelines to follow?

• Use frames if they help the user, not just because you like them.

• Make the dynamic frame the largest one.

• Keep the overall number of frames to a minimum. Each one reduces the space within each frame.

• Keep the number of static frames to the minimum number you need to provide adequate navigation.

• If you use a 17" or 21" monitor to develop pages you are lucky. Remember that most users will be using 14" or 15" monitors. This makes a big difference in readability.

• If you want to delete a framed page, you must delete the frameset and all the target pages.

• Although you can make one of the files that goes into a frame a frameset itself, making an individual frame contain its own frames, this may make the page too full of information.

**Use the tools to create your page**

Having thought through all the issues to do with colours, typefaces and graphics, you can now start to lay out your pages. The first thing to do is to create the standard features for each page.

## Set up navigation controls

One of the biggest problems users find when working through hyperlink-type material is getting lost. Users need to have buttons or text that they can click to take them forwards or backwards. They need to have visual clues on each page that tell them where they are. Making navigation easy and obvious is therefore vitally important for an intranet designer.

What navigational controls do you need? You need to make sure that, wherever they are, the user knows where they are and where they can go. This table shows you how you can make sure they can answer both of those questions with a yes.

| | How you can do it |
|---|---|
| **Where am I?** | When you create a web page, your HTML editor will ask you to give the page a title. This is picked up by the browser and will appear at the very top of the browser window. The page title is also the part of the file that web search engines scan and index. If you want your intranet's search engine to make a record of your page, make sure that you do give it a title and that this describes what the page is all about. <br><br> Follow these guidelines for titling the page: <br> • Give it a title! <br> • Describe what the page contains <br> • Show how it relates to other pages on the web <br><br> For example, think about the pages for the surveyors. Suitable page titles for this web could be: <br><br> `Classifying structural details: age` <br> `Classifying structural details: built form` <br> `Classifying structural details: solar access factor` <br> `Classifying structural details: house volume` <br> `etc.` <br><br> Also use titles within the text on the page itself that show the user what page they are on and indicate how this page links in with other pages. |

| **Where can I go?** | Each page needs to have specific navigational controls that guide the user through the logical sequence of screens, and general controls that give the user the chance to go back to, for example: |

• the home page of that part of the web

• key parts of the rest of the intranet

Consider first the specific controls. These must identify clearly the content of the previous and next pages. Do not just use 'Back' or 'Next'. Think about this user, who is working through Pages A, B and C:

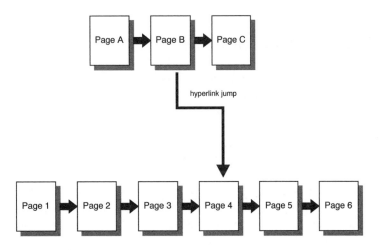

*Figure 7.3 Dangers of relying on 'Back' commands*

On Page B they see a link that takes them to Page 4. If they see a control there that says 'Back' does that mean Page 3 or Page B? If they want to return to Page B, they can use the 'Back' button on their browser. If they want to delve backwards through Pages 3, 2 and 1 they use the specific control on the page itself.

The general controls you build in will depend on the features you have within your intranet, but typically they might be:

• the intranet home page, so that users can always leap back to the start

• search facilities – your intranet will probably have software that allows the user to look for keywords

• index – you may have a master index of all the main home pages stored on the system

• staff directory - at any time people may want to find a phone or room number

You can provide these navigational controls in one of two ways. You could type in the text 'Intranet Home Page' and set up the link, but there is a danger that the user will not see this text clearly among all the other text.

The best thing to do is create a small graphic file that represents the Home Page and set this up as a hyperlink. This is much clearer to the user and should be more attractive. Sometimes a line of such general navigational links are placed on a single graphic file that runs horizontally across or vertically down the page. Called a *buttonbar*, this is a good example of an imagemap: different parts of the image carry links to different pages.

Whether you use graphical buttons or text, *be consistent about where you put them*. Decide they will go at the top of the page or at the bottom, or both. What will get users really confused are pages where these general navigation buttons could be anywhere!

## Add the editorial features

What are the editorial features you need? This is basically *who owns the page*, i.e. who looks after it. Users may want to contact you to let you know about something wrong or that could be improved. Make sure they can do that by giving your name and contact number.

Also add the date when the page was first posted and the date of the last revision. This is important so that users know how up to date the page is.

Follow these guidelines to help you put your pages together. But do not worry about getting everything absolutely right first time. The beauty about an intranet is that you can quickly and easily make changes based on what users tell you. We shall look at how to do that effectively in Chapter 9.

## Lay out the text

You can now start to think about adding text to the page. Many of the principles of good page design on paper also apply to web page design. In particular, you need to keep a careful eye on the amount of text and its relationship to graphical images.

In this respect HTML does you few favours. The original designers of HTML did not imagine that people would want to use it to develop sophisticated graphic designs. They saw it as an essentially utilitarian tool and set up the language so that, for example, by default text automatically flows out to fill the width of the window. As we saw in Chapter 2, reading long lines is harder on the eyes than reading short lines, so it is useful to have some way of forcing the lines to stay the same length. Therefore what you need to do is to find ways of getting around these limitations to get the page layouts you want.

To achieve this you will need to use tables. They are arguably the most useful feature within HTML as far as text layout is concerned. Arranging text and graphics in tabular form gives you a lot of extra flexibility in page design. Don't be misled by the name 'table': while you can use them to show conventional tabular data, the most common way in which tables are used is to arrange pages of text. For example, you can:

- arrange a menu list in individual cells to give a columnar look – this will allow you to present more options on a page without the user having to scroll up or down

- insert graphics into cells, so that you can arrange a graphic and its supporting text side by side

These are possibilities because you can decide whether or not to show the table borders. You might want to show the outlines if you are using the table in a conventional way to display tabular information. Otherwise it is generally considered good practice to hide the borders. One practical reason for this is that, as we saw with bullets, different browsers display table borders differently.

You can also:

- make any text or graphic in a cell a hyperlink

- insert a table within the cell of another table

How easy it is to create tables depends on your HTML skills or the power of your HTML editor. However, if you have worked with tables in a word processor, you will know that they can be frustrating things to work with if you need to resize them or add and remove cells. It is similar with HTML editors, so it is a good idea to sketch out on paper what you want to go into the table before you start on screen. This can save a lot of frustration!

We can next see how to lay out some of the material from our case studies using tables. Although we shall be using the FrontPage Editor to do this layout work, it is beyond the scope of this book to explain in detail how to use FrontPage. There are a number of excellent books available (some listed in the bibliography) that can help to fill in the gaps that this chapter leaves.

You would first choose the colour scheme to follow. In this case we are going to use a simple combination of black text on a grey background. This is a practical combination that gives good contrast and makes reading easier.

In Chapter 6 we wrote the raw text for the pages on windows. We saved this as ASCII text and can now paste that into the FrontPage editor.

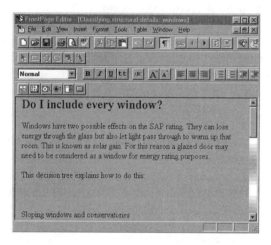

*Figure 7.4: Raw text in the FrontPage Editor*

You can see that we have set the heading format already, in this case to Heading 2. Let us see what happens when we load this page into a browser:

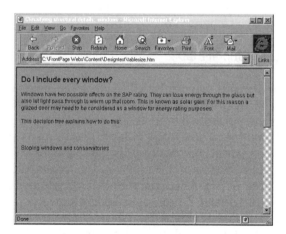

*Figure 7.5: Raw text displayed in the browser*

The text has flowed out to fill the browser window, and is really too wide for comfortable reading. Let us now put this text into a table to fix the width.

1. Click the cursor where you want the table to appear.

2. Select Table, Insert Table.

3. You can now set the table properties. The ones we are interested in here are:
    • Columns – set this to 1
    • Alignment – set this to Left
    • Width – check the Specify width box, select 'in Pixels' and type '400' into the box

Your screen would then look like this:

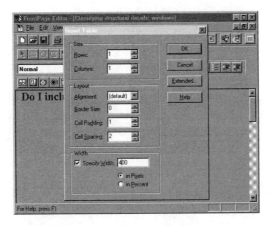

*Figure 7.6: Creating a fixed width table*

What have you done? You have created a one row, one column table with a fixed size. HTML calls this an absolute size, as it means that whatever width the browser window is, the table will always be 400 pixels wide. If you chose to specify the width in terms of a percentage, it would shrink and grow with the size of the browser window, taking the text with it. This can be a useful feature, but not if we want to fix the text layout. We have chosen 400 pixels, as this represents about 60% of the width of a standard 640 x 480 VGA screen, which is likely to be the lowest common denominator screen resolution.

This would give a line length that would allow about 8–12 words, which is good for reading. You cannot know this precisely, as it depends on the size the user has set for their normal text. In the screens on the next page the text is 10pt; 12pt text would reduce the line length by about two words.

Now look at the difference between the same page in a narrow and a wide browser window:

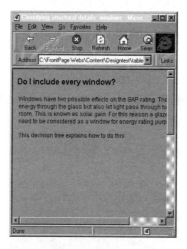

*Figure 7.7: The fixed width table displayed in a narrow browser window*

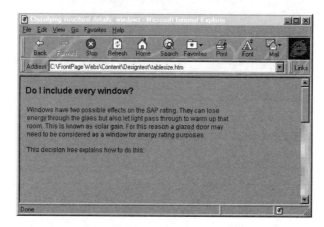

*Figure 7.8: The fixed width table displayed in a wide browser window*

You can see that the text stays with the same layout and does not flow out.

You can refine this table layout further by giving the table two columns. When you do this you have to realise that, although your table is an absolute size, individual cells are by default relative. This means that a cell will shrink to almost nothing if it is empty and a cell with lots of text will expand. You should therefore set up all cells as absolute. To do this:

1. Click inside the cell you want to fix.

2. Right click and the properties window pops up.

3. Select Cell Properties.

4. Check Specify Width, select 'in Pixels' and type in the number you want the cell to fill, in this case 50.

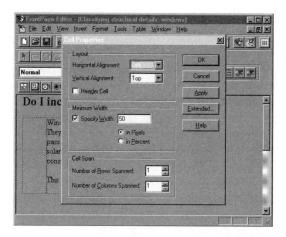

*Figure 7.9: Fixing the width of individual cells*

There are some other features about tables that you can see in this dialogue box. You can use this box to change the alignment of objects within a cell, both vertically and horizontally. Also notice the wording 'minimum width'. This is because what you are actually specifying here is the smallest the cell can be; it can grow if you put something bigger into it, such as an image.

This page would then look like this:

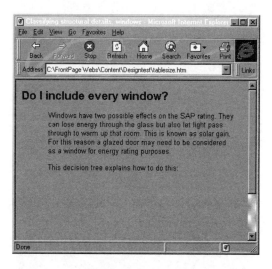

*Figure 7.10: Fixed width table and cells displaying text*

In this case we just have a wide left-hand margin, but you could insert an image into the left-hand column if you wanted. This is how you can get more control over bulleted lists: design a bullet point and save it as a small image file, then paste it into the left-hand column.

A disadvantage with this method is that browsers that are not loading graphics will see the standard browser symbol rather than your bullet.

The next task is to insert a graphic of the decision tree. We can create this graphic in any package we want, as long as we can then convert it into a GIF or a JPG file. However, be careful about the size of the image: work out before you start what the width of the image must be in pixels, as if you have to reduce it to fit into the browser window you will lose some definition. For this reason you may find it easier to use graphics packages that are specially designed for producing web graphics, such as Paint Shop Pro. This package lets you specify the pixel size of the image you want to create.

To insert the image:

1. Click your cursor at the point where you want the graphic to go.

2. Select Insert, Image, then choose the file you want.

3. Click on OK and the graphic appears.

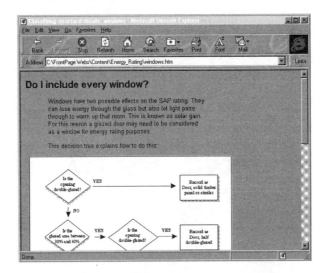

*Figure 7.11: Using a GIF with an opaque background*

This shows what the page looks like with an opaque GIF file. You can improve the look of the page by making the background colour in the image file transparent.

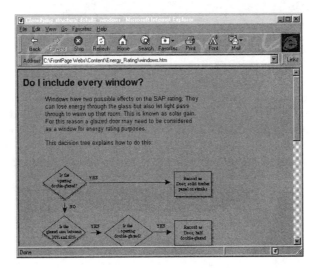

*Figure 7.12: Using a GIF with a transparent background*

How to Design and Post Information on a Corporate Intranet

Next add the general navigational features to the page. We shall do it here using a type of imagemap called a buttonbar. This has icons and some text representing the other pages to which the user can jump. You need to decide where you are going to place this bar: at the top, bottom or along the side? You can ask users to help you decide which is the best place. Wherever you do put it, be consistent.

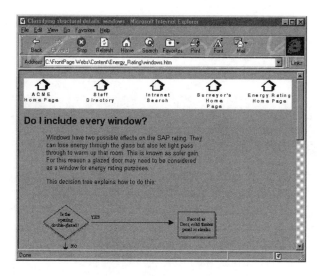

*Figure 7.13: Using a buttonbar for navigational controls*

We now need to convert this graphic into an imagemap, by creating hotspots that can set up a hyperlink between each icon and its relevant page. It is very easy to do this in FrontPage:

1. Select the buttonbar image.

2. Click on the rectangle on the toolbar.

3. Point the cursor at the top left-hand corner of your chosen hotspot area, hold the left mouse button down and drag it out to cover the icon.

4. Release it and choose the target for the hyperlink from the dialogue box that appears.

Repeat this for each icon, then add the page-specific navigational details. This will be to allow the user to go back to the previous page and forward to the next page. We could do this using images, but as we would have to create different ones for every page it will be much easier to provide this navigation through appropriately worded text. To make it distinct from the rest of the text, we can use a horizontal line to show an end to the text above.

1. Move the cursor to the line below the image and click.

2. Select Insert, Horizontal Line.

This inserts a line with default properties, 2 pixels thick, centred and filling 100% of the window. By right clicking on the line you can change any of these properties.

Type the text you want under the line, and you can then add the hyperlink.

1. Select the text you want to activate the link, in this case we shall use 'wall characteristics'.

2. Click on the link button (the one that looks like a chain).

3. Select the page to which you want the link to go.

Your page now has all its basic features. Save the file and look in the FrontPage Explorer to see if your linkages are all there. You repeat this process for each page and slowly the web will develop.

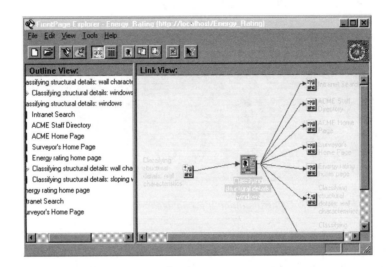

*Figure 7.14: Using FrontPage Explorer to show the page hyperlinks*

## How to design the site using frames

We might want to design the site to incorporate frames. FrontPage makes this relatively easy. We shall design a site that has three frames:

- a static frame with intranet navigational controls
- a static frame with energy rating site controls
- a dynamic frame with the actual information

1. Open the FrontPage Editor and create the first three files. These are called:

- ACME Navigation, which will be the intranet navigation frame with just a buttonbar graphic.

- Energy Navigation, which is the energy rating site navigation controller. It has the text below:

    **How to assess the energy characteristics of domestic properties**

    How to classify:

    - structural details
    - fuels
    - space heating systems
    - heating systems control types
    - water heating systems
    - pumps, fans and ventilation

- Information, which is the first page to appear in the dynamic frame. This simply says:

    **How to assess the energy characteristics of domestic properties**

2. Again in FrontPage Editor, select, File, New and choose the Frames Wizard.

3. Follow the on-screen instructions so that you have a grid like this:

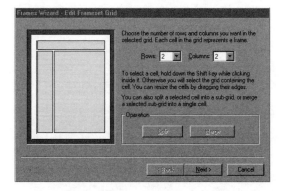

*Figure 7.15: Using the Frames Wizard to lay out the frameset*

4. Select each frame in turn. Give each a name, such as Topstatic, Leftstatic and Dynamic, and enter the URL of the first page to go in each one.

5. Select the top static frame. Set Scrolling to 'no' and check Not resizable.

6. Select the left static frame. Set scrolling to 'auto' and leave the Not resizable box unchecked.

7. Click the Edit button and you return to the Editor.

8. Click on File, Page properties. Type 'Dynamic' into the Default Target Frame box. This is identifying the dynamic frame as the place where hyperlinks selected from this frame will be displayed. You can allow resizing and scrolling in these frames.

9. Repeat for the dynamic frame, typing 'Dynamic' in the Default box. This is the file that will be loaded into the dynamic frame after this first page.

10. Click Next for each screen that follows. You can ignore the warnings that may appear for now, although when you are developing a real-life site you will have to resolve these issues.

11. Save all the files in the Editor, and load this frameset file into your browser. It should look something like this:

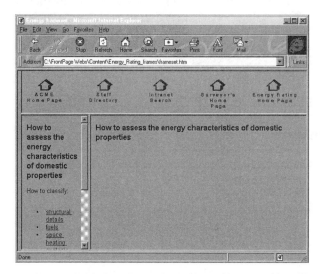

*Figure 7.16: The framed site*

If you click on the structural details hyperlink, a sub-menu appears in the dynamic frame. The user can then click on hyperlinks here for the page they want.

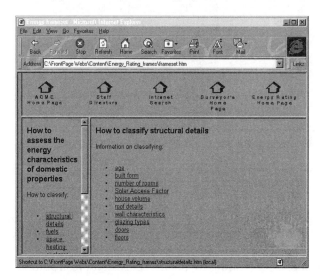

*Figure 7.17: Using the framed site*

When you create hyperlinks, make sure you type the name of the frame where you want the page to be loaded in the Target Frame box.

If the user clicks on the buttonbar, they will go off to the appropriate page elsewhere in the intranet, which may or may not be framed.

That, briefly, is how to create a framed page with our information on energy rating. FrontPage takes a lot of the pain out of the process, but it can still be exasperating. However, you can see how it improves the usability of the site. Before deciding to use frames, however, do consider the constraints outlined earlier in this chapter.

## Key points from the chapter

- Decide in general terms how to integrate backgrounds, graphics and text so that the site gives you the effect you want.

- Decide whether you are going to design a framed site.

- Make sure each page tells the user:

    - where they are

    - where they can go

- Lay out the text, keeping in mind the advantages of using tables to fix the text.

# Chapter 8

# How to build interactivity into your site

# Chapter 8
## How to build interactivity into your site

After reading this chapter you will be able to:

- decide how to integrate questions into intranet-based information systems

- write effective questions

 **What is interactivity?**

> '**interact** – act reciprocally, act on each other', from the *Concise Oxford Dictionary*

That is a dictionary definition of the word. By this measure there is some degree of interactivity between a user and an intranet site. Each page presents a number of possibilities to the user in terms of moving on, and the user makes a decision. However, this is somewhat limited, and real interactivity only comes when the user is directly asked to make a decision which has some potential for a right or wrong answer. If we want to make this happen we start to move into the area of computer-based training (CBT).

CBT is a big area, and I do not intend to start a discussion here about how to design such materials. It is certainly possible to deliver large-scale training programmes across an intranet, albeit with certain technical constraints about the type of media that you can use. It also means that you have to start to use different software tools, as simple HTML is not capable of producing the type of functionality that CBT needs.

However, what we can think about here is how to enhance information delivery across your intranet by adding in simple questions. Let us first look at some models that can illustrate how to integrate information delivery with training.

## 1. The computer-based training model.

This is the traditional way in which CBT courses are designed, as a tutorial which integrates information provision with self-assessment questions. It is often the most obvious way to design courses, possibly because it is similar to what we remember from our own experiences of education: the teacher gives us information then asks us questions about it.

However, at its most simple level it can be tedious for the user, as it can seem like a trudge through endless screens. It also means that all users work through the same material, regardless of their existing levels of knowledge and skill.

The basic model can be improved to make it more flexible and interesting, but it still fails to make full use of an intranet's capabilities.

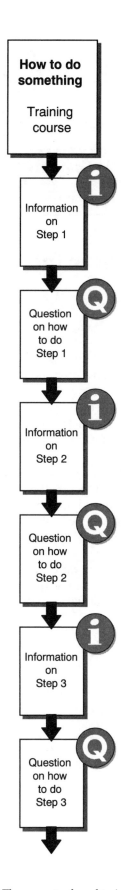

*Figure 8.1: The computer-based training model*

## 2. The just-in-time model

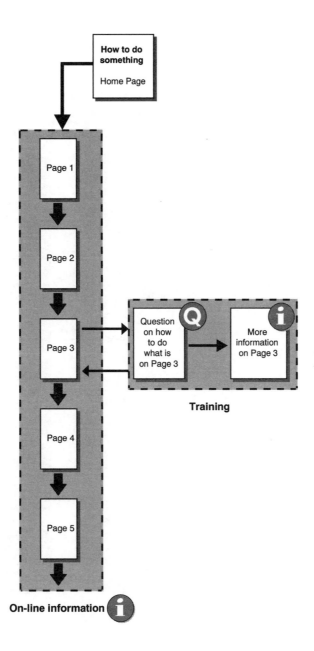

*Figure 8.2: The just-in-time model*

The JIT model is based on what this book has already looked at in some detail. We provide the user with the key information on how to do the task, then provide opportunities for them to answer questions on each step where we think it is relevant.

For example, think about the energy rating of domestic properties case study. In Chapters 6 and 7 we drafted some text about classifying windows. We could supplement this with questions which give the user some specific windows to classify. This would mean that they work through the decision trees to check that they can use them correctly.

This is probably the simplest model for you to work with if you are not experienced in designing computer-based training materials.

## 3. The on-line model

The on-line model is really an integration of the first two models, and is the one that harnesses the power of the intranet most effectively.

It separates out pure training from information. The training side could present questions about specific examples of this step in the process. The questions could all be linked as part of a case study.

Instead of the user working through information then routinely answering a question, they can choose to:

- work through just the information, then if they want to check their understanding they can access a relevant question

- follow the training side, and access further information on each step as they need

This provides much greater flexibility and caters for the different ways in which people like to learn. Some people like to gather all the information first, then try it out. Others like to try things out first, making mistakes and then finding the information they need to get it right.

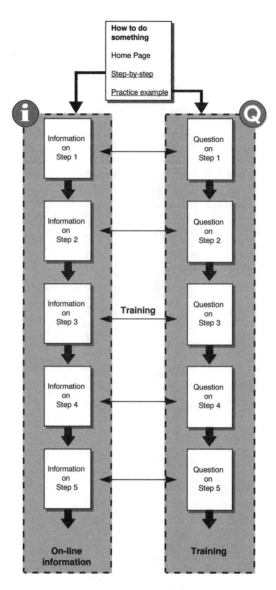

Figure 8.3: The on-line model

Of these three, the JIT and on-line models are those that will be of most use to you when designing information systems. They provide the greatest degree of flexibility for the user and cater for the different needs of everyone within the target group.

It is relatively easy to move from the CBT model to the JIT model by separating information and questioning. Make the information linear and provide hyperlinks to questions related to that specific page as appropriate.

If you are unfamiliar with designing computer-based training you may find it difficult at first to produce information and training that corresponds to the on-line model. After all, this is a skill and needs practice. But if you think about the processes we have followed in this book, particularly how to use pyramid analysis to break down a process into its sub-tasks, you will see how you can adapt them to develop both information and training.

# What are the technological issues?

This may all sound straightforward. However, as soon as we try to put it into practice we run into a problem: HTML does not cater for designing interactive questioning. You can in theory use hyperlinking to write multiple choice questions: the user clicks on the answer they think correct, and a page loads that gives feedback. However, they would lose the original page or part of the page. You could use frames with a question in a static frame and an answer in a dynamic frame, but the programming effort to do this would be considerable and the end result would still not be particularly elegant. Remember that most people in large organisations have used some form of computer-based training and will be familiar with clever screen designs and sophisticated effects. They will not be impressed by what you can achieve with straight HTML even though you may think that it is a very clever piece of programming!

You will also run into problems if you want to have the server keep a record of how each user answers questions. Once the server has sent the page data to the user's computer it breaks off the connection. If you want the user's answer to be stored, you have to design special programs that will make a connection to the server, identify the user, open a database file, then enter the data about the response. That is difficult to do for a non-specialist programmer.

However, new developments in programming are rapidly making it possible for non-programmers to overcome these problems. These fall into two areas:

- *Plugins* – training is programmed in special authoring software, and the server and browser each use special software that can package up these non-HTML files into a format that the browser can read and display.

- *Java* – a special programming language that can run executable files on the borrower's host computer.

## Traditional authoring systems and plugins

There are a number of software packages available that have been specifically designed to create interactive training. These include IconAuthor, Authorware and Multimedia Toolbook, and they are used routinely to create computer-based training programmes that may include multimedia. A training designer can produce tutorial materials and interactive questioning, and also set up management systems that will store information on a user's responses. These packages all, to a greater or lesser extent, let non-programmers produce sophisticated training programs.

Latest releases of these are now being described as 'Internet ready' – what does that mean?

Essentially what 'Internet ready' packages do is to provide what is called a 'plugin' for the user's browser. This is a software addition to the browser that recognises and interprets specific types of file sent to it. One part of the plugin program sits on the server alongside the web server software and the normal HTML files. When the authoring system's files are called by the browser, it packages the program up into a suitable format and sends it down to the browser. The plugin interprets the file and plays it just as if it were an ordinary HTML file.

There are a large number of different plugins available for different purposes. Two examples are:

- Shockwave – a plugin that lets users run Macromedia Director and Authorware programs

- RealAudio – a plugin that lets users download an audio file and hear it as it is being sent down the network

While this technique does work quite effectively, it represents a step away from the intranet's ability to deliver all types of information to one interface: if someone wants to access the file they have to have the plugin. The Authorware plugin will not be able to read IconAuthor files, for example. In a corporate setting it may not be too difficult to make sure that everyone has the right plugins, but it does represent yet another issue for network administrators to consider. There may also be significant licensing costs for the use of the plugins.

The effectiveness of the plugins also varies. In some cases the server may bundle up a very large file to send, which will take a considerable time to download. Other programs only bundle up small parts at a time. Some programs will check to see if there is a plugin installed on the browser, and if there isn't will install it automatically, but some will not.

This is today's technology as far as non-programmers trying to deliver interactive training over an intranet is concerned. However, it is rapidly being superseded by what is becoming the hottest programming language around, Java.

## Java, the way forward

Java is a new programming language designed specifically for web-based systems. It follows the same principles as HTML: the server sends the file down and the browser decides how to display it. How it does this will vary according to whether the browser is on a PC, Mac or UNIX workstation. The difference with Java is that the data sent down is actually an executable program, called an 'applet', rather than just page layout information. The browser executes the file in a way that is appropriate for its own operating system. It then disappears and does not stay on the receiving computer. This assumes that the browser can deal with the Java file: latest versions of Netscape and Internet Explorer are 'Java-enabled' and can.

Java is therefore the first programming language whose files can really work on any type of computer. It is the programming reality behind the 'network computer' concept: if the bandwidth of the link from the server to the computer were big enough, you could receive a whole word processor or spreadsheet application, use it then lose it. That is some way in the future, but is a real possibility, limited only by today's inability to send data fast enough. It will not be a restriction for long.

How might this work for delivering interactive training today? One example could be to design a multiple choice question and program it in Java. The server would send it down when asked and the browser would execute the file. The user would answer the question, see the feedback, and the program would send information on the user's response back to the server for storage. The file would then disappear.

Therefore all we need is a Java programmer and we could do it. If you can program in Java yourself or you know somebody who can, use this method. It is the way of the future and will soon supersede the plugin technologies. However, at the moment there are no tools available for non-programmers that have anything like the functionality of something like IconAuthor or Authorware. There is a tool called Jamba, made by the same company that developed IconAuthor, that allows non-programmers to prepare Java-based presentations through a drag-and-drop WYSIWYG interface, but it does not have all the features that interactive training designs call for. However, within the next eighteen months it probably will.

 # What sorts of questions are there?

Questions present the user with an immediate decision about a specific problem. You can use questions to:

- let the user check their understanding of the contents of the page

- test that they do know the contents, and direct them through other information as necessary

- stimulate the user to think about a subject before exploring it in more detail

- manage navigation – instead of providing answers, you let the user's response take them to another part of the training

Whatever the purpose, there are some standard questioning techniques you can use.

## 1. Multiple choice questions

These are the favourites for computer-based questioning, mainly because it is easy to program the computer to mark them. However, they are probably the hardest sort of question to write because it is usually difficult to find enough plausible wrong answers (called 'distracters'). You have to make sure that nothing in the way the answers are written suggests that one is correct or another is obviously incorrect. Think about multiple choice tests and quizzes you have done. Have you ever been able to work out most of the correct answers by guessing? The 'check your personality' quizzes in popular magazines are examples of this. You will usually know what sort of overall result you are looking for, and, unless you are very honest and strong-willed, it can be very easy to pick the answers that will give you the answer you want.

Multiple choice questions do not have to be text based. You can ask the user to select the correct diagram or photograph, or you can use image maps and ask them to click on the correct part of the image.

Whichever method you use, here are some guidelines that will help you design effective multiple choice questions:

| | |
|---|---|
| **Offer four possible answers** | The more alternatives there are, the harder it is for the user to guess the right answer, but the harder it gets for you to come up with plausible distracters! Four possible answers is the best compromise. |
| **Make all the choices plausible** | If you have written multiple choice questions before you will know that thinking of the first distracter is easy, the second is fairly difficult and the third can be almost impossible. Accept that it will take a long time to write a good question, and do not add any distracters that are obviously incorrect just to finish the question. Also resist the temptation to put one in as a joke. It merely increases the user's chance of guessing the right answer from those left. For example:<br><br>`In network language, 'IP' stands for:`<br>`1. Internal Processing`<br>`2. Internet Protocol`<br>`3. Important Protocol`<br>`4. Internal Protocol`<br><br>Is answer 3 plausible? |

| | |
|---|---|
| **Present a clear problem to the user** | Avoid questions that are vague and can mean different things to different people. For example:<br><br>```<br>What is the most useful chapter in this book?<br>1.Chapter 1<br>2.Chapter 3<br>3.Chapter 4<br>4.Chapter 6<br>```<br><br>Different people will have found different chapters most interesting. Also, what about the people who thought that Chapter 5 was the best? |
| **Keep as much information as possible in the stem** | The stem is the first part of the question. To follow this guideline we would rewrite the question above as:<br><br>```<br>The most useful chapter in this book is:<br>1.   1<br>2.   3<br>3.   4<br>4.   6<br>``` |
| **Avoid putting in clues** | There are many ways of giving a user clues. Look out for:<br><br>• ending the stem with 'an' and offering only one answer that begins with a vowel (obvious but easy to do!)<br>• making the right answer the longest, which you may feel forced to do to in order to define it so tightly that it is definitely the right answer<br>• one option number being used regularly for the right answer |
| **Do not ask the user to say which is not an answer** | Think about this question:<br><br>```<br>Which of the following software packages is not in Microsoft Office?<br>1.Excel<br>2.PowerPoint<br>3.Project<br>4.Word<br>```<br><br>When you try to answer this question your thought processes go something like: 'Well, Excel, PowerPoint and Word are in Office, so ... Is that the right answer? No, so Project must be.' What happens is that it becomes a test of reasoning rather than on knowledge of Microsoft Office. Also it focuses interest of the wrong answers rather than the right one. |

| | |
|---|---|
| **Do not use 'none' or 'all' as a possible answer** | Think about this question:<br><br>```\nWhich one of the following software packages\nis in Microsoft Office?\n1.Excel\n2.Symphony\n3.WordPerfect\n4.All of these\n```<br><br>If the user knows that WordPerfect *is not* in Office, then 'All' cannot be a possible answer. The answer is therefore a guess between two options. |
| **Keep answers in alphabetical or numerical order where appropriate** | If the possible answers are single words or numbers, put them in order. |

Following these guidelines will help you to design better multiple choice questions. Do not underestimate the time taken to write these questions: you could realistically spend an hour writing a well-designed multiple choice question.

Here is a tip you may find useful if you find it hard to think up distracters:

1. Write on paper your basic questions without any answers, and allow some space for the users to write their answers.

2. Get a panel of typical users together and ask them to answer the questions.

3. Collect in the papers and use the wrong answers to give you distracters. As real people thought they were correct, they must be plausible!

## 2. Matching questions

These are an enhancement to the basic multiple choice type. Essentially they combine several multiple choice questions in one.

For example:

```
Match the car to the maker:

   1.Ford        A.Astra
   2.Vauxhall    B.216
   3.Rover       C.Escort
   4.Jaguar      D.Primera
                 E.XJ-S
```

These are useful questions as they can test a lot of information within one question, but they can suffer from similar weaknesses in design as do multiple choice questions.

Guidelines to follow:

| | |
|---|---|
| **Keep the instructions simple** | It can be hard to write instructions that are short and easy to follow. One way to keep the instructions easier is to use numbers for one list and letters for the other, as above. |
| **Keep each list homogeneous** | Make each list contain the same sort of item. In the example above, the first list is of car makers and the second models. |
| **Avoid clues** | Avoid items in the lists that can only possibly go with particular items in the other list. For example:<br><br>```Match each item of medical equipment`<br>`with its function:`<br>`1.Thermometer   A.Cuts tissue`<br>`2.Scalpel       B.Holds tissue`<br>`3.Forceps       C.Listens to heart`<br>`                  beat`<br>`4.Stethoscope   D.Measures temperature`<br>`                E.Looks inside the eye```<br><br>The first list has just one measuring device, and the second list just one measurement function. |
| **Make the second list longer than the first** | If the lists are the same length, the user may be able to work out the answer to the last on the list by having eliminated all the other possible answers. Keeping the second list longer ensures uncertainty. |

## 3. Alternative response questions

These are a specialised type of multiple choice question with only two possible answers, for example 'Yes/No', 'Up/Down'. Do not use them out of choice, as there is a 50% chance of guessing the right answer, but you may need to use them in cases where there genuinely are only two possible answers.

Keep the guidelines for multiple choice questions in mind, to avoid increasing the chances of a right guess.

## 4. Free format questions

These questions simply ask the user to put their answer to the question in a space. For example:

```
What is Ford's large family car called:
```

The problem with this is how to mark it. If you are marking by hand it is easier, but if the computer is doing it you have to make sure that it can recognise misspellings and incorrect capitalisation. In this example, you would probably have to make sure that 'mondeo', 'mondo', 'Mondo', 'It is the Mondeo', etc. were all accepted by the computer.

For this reason it is not generally a good idea to include this sort of question in computer-based training materials. They are however, very good at testing someone's understanding of a subject, as they offer the lowest possible chance of guessing the right answer.

One instance where they can be used relatively safely is for numerical answers. For example:

```
Above a certain pitch you must classify a window as a roof
light.  What pitch is this (in degrees)?
```

This is as safe as this sort of question can be. Even so, someone may choose to type in 'seventy'!

Let us now see how we can design a question for the surveyors' case study and incorporate this into a web page. We shall use AimTech's IconAuthor to do this.

Consider the page on classifying windows. The surveyor needs to be able to use this flowchart:

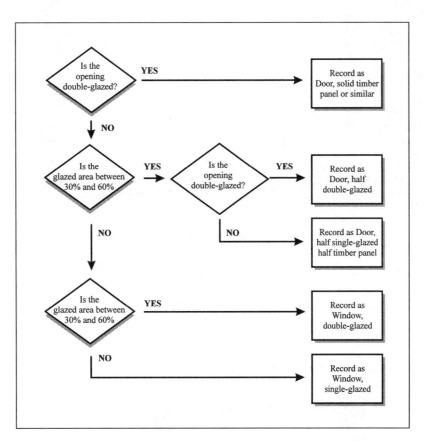

*Figure 8.4: Surveyor's flowchart for classifying windows*

You could therefore design a question that tests this. The following question would be suitable:

```
You find a door that has a single-glazed window that occupies
60% of the door area.  How would you classify it:

1.Door, solid timber panel or similar

2.Door, half single-glazed, half timber panel

3.Window, single-glazed
```

There are only three options because there are only three plausible answers for this particular door.

Having prepared the wording for the question you can use IconAuthor to develop the question. This shows some of the flowcharting within IconAuthor that will run this question:

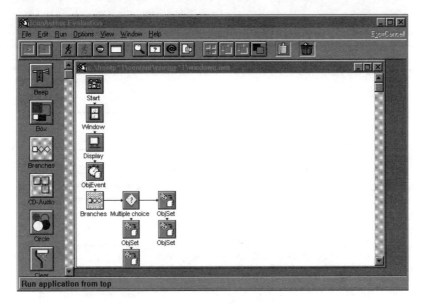

*Figure 8.5: IconAuthor flowchart*

Test this file within IconAuthor to check that it works, then you can integrate it into your site.

1.  The next step is to create a link from your web page to this file.

2.  Open the relevant file in FrontPage Editor.

3.  Add a line of text that will serve as your hyperlink.

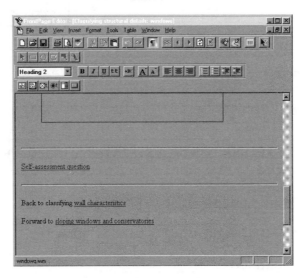

*Figure 8.6: Hypertext link for the question*

1.  Highlight the text and click on the Link button.

2.  Select Current Web and type in the name of the IconAuthor file. FrontPage may query this as it does not expect files of this type, but ignore this.

3.  Save the file.

You next need to make sure that the IconAuthor plugin is installed in the browser. This should be a straightforward installation process using your IconAuthor disks. When you have done that, you can check that the link works by loading the HTML page and clicking on the hyperlink.

You would see the page below. You can then answer the question just as if it were a stand-alone computer-based training application:

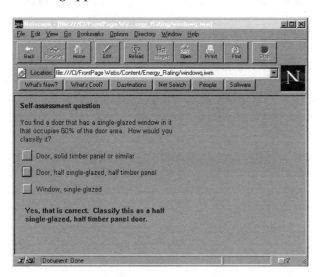

*Figure 8.7: The IconAuthor question in the browser*

This shows you that it is quite easy to incorporate questioning into a web site, providing you have the right software in which to author it and the skill to use it.

You can of course use IconAuthor to develop much larger and more sophisticated training packages that can be delivered in their entirety across your intranet. These would allow you to do more complex things, such as store details about users' responses for future analysis. However, as we have seen here, it is also possible to use it if you are simply designing information and want to add some questions at appropriate points.

# Key points from the chapter

- Adding questions improves the quality of the user's interaction with the site.

- You cannot rely on HTML alone to develop questions for the user to answer.

- Plugins allow you to link material authored in non-HTML applications to your site.

- Java can allow you to develop sophisticated interactivity.

- Questions can be as hard to write as to answer.

- With the right software it is relatively easy to incorporate questions in a web site.

# Chapter

# 9

# How to make sure you develop a quality site

How to Design and Post Information on a Corporate Intranet

# Chapter 9
## How to make sure you develop a quality site

After reading this chapter you will be able to:

> • prepare a quality management plan for the development of your site
>
> • use your project team to develop an error-free product that meets the users' needs

What is quality? That is the subject of a motorcycle ride across the United States and book in its own right, so can do little but scratch the surface here. A dictionary definition can help:

*'quality – the degree of excellence of a thing', from the* Concise Oxford Dictionary

So what is going to make your site excellent? Here is a list of ideas:

• *Usefulness* – people use it because they find it helps them

• *Style* – it looks good and there are no typographical mistakes, misspellings or grammatical errors

• *Programming* – it works technically, with no dead-end pages and no faulty hyperlinks

This will be the USP of your site. There is a jargon term used in selling, the Unique Selling Proposition, which is what makes your product so much better than anyone else's. Your USP means something different, but it is also what is going to make your site that much better than anyone else's.

You may be able to think of more measurements of quality, but I think that these cover the key measures of quality for a web site. Any process that you follow to maintain quality must cover these issues. Do not think that getting two out of three is good enough either. It may be well structured and look great, but if users find technical problems with it they will soon stop using it. Quality control therefore has to be comprehensive.

The quality process must also start on Day One of the project. It is no good waiting until all the screens are developed then make the changes you need to satisfy the three criteria. It will probably take you at least twice as long as you have already spent on the project up to that point if you add quality at the end. Build quality in from the beginning.

To do this you must think of yourself as a project manager. We looked at this in Chapter 3, where we first discussed how important it is to follow a project-based approach. In that chapter we looked at how to assemble a project team, with high performers, subject matter experts and representatives from the target group. That is an important part of the quality process as these people will play important roles in developing the quality. In this chapter we shall see how to build in the quality to your site by making sure that the three criteria are continually being considered.

# The quality process

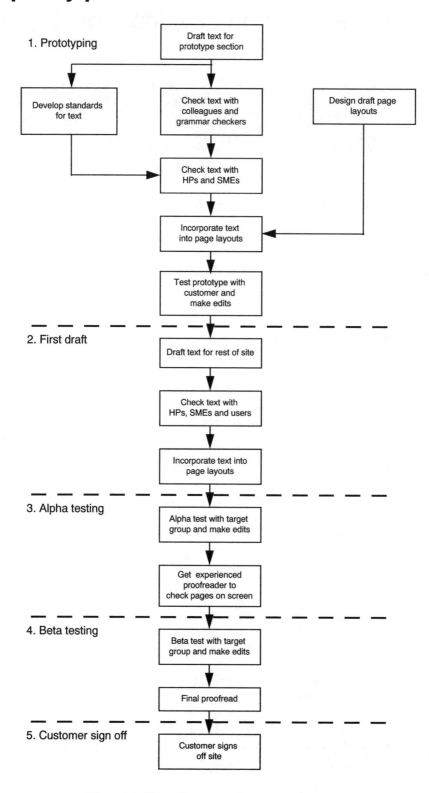

*Figure 9.1: The quality process for web site development*

This flowchart shows how you can split the design and development process up into five stages. We shall look at each one in turn.

## Stage 1 – Prepare a prototype

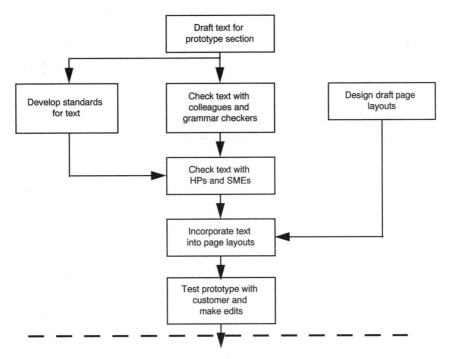

*Figure 9.2: Prototyping*

Prototyping allows you to develop a small part of the site, test it out with key people and make changes. It will save you from developing most of the site and then finding that there are some fundamental flaws in the design. It will also give you a chance to work through the design and development process and see what unexpected problems there are.

Decide which part of the site you will use as the prototype. The first section is an obvious choice, but make sure that it is representative of the site as a whole. If you think most of the site will be dependent on good quality graphics, do not choose a section that has few graphics just because it is the first.

We shall work through each of these steps, considering how they cover the three criteria. By the end of the stage we will have considered each well enough for us to feel confident about going on to the next stage.

## Draft text for prototype section

You start to write for the target group, making sure that the level of the language is correct as far as you can know at this stage.

| Usability | |
|---|---|
| Style | ✓ |
| Programming | |

Do not think that everything must be 100% right before you let anyone else look at it. If you do, you will end up spending hours working away trying to get the last little bits right. Remember the 80:20 rule, which in this case means that you can spend 80% of the time trying to fill in the last 20% of the content! Instead, plan to get 80% right in 20% of the time, then fill in the gaps when you show the text to high performers and subject matter experts.

## Develop standards for text

Building on any existing standards, you develop a set of standards covering spellings, punctuation, grammatical issues, etc.

| Usability | |
|---|---|
| Style | |
| Programming | ✓ |

This will be an organic document as far as spellings are concerned. When you come across a word with potentially alternative spellings, decide what you are going to do with it and add it to the list. Circulate the list to anyone else working on the project. A project site on your intranet would be an ideal way of sharing this information.

## Check text with colleagues and grammar checkers

When you feel that you have put in everything you can:

| Usability | ✓ |
|---|---|
| Style | ✓ |
| Programming | |

- pass it through a spell and grammar checker

- let colleagues read through it

Colleagues will give you the first feedback on the language and how well they think it might work.

## Check text with HPs and SMEs

The high performers are the ones who know a lot about the practicalities of the subject already and the subject matter experts know the detail, so they will be able to comment on the accuracy and completeness of the material.

| Usability | ✓ |
|---|---|
| Style | |
| Programming | |

## Develop page layouts

Experiment with different page designs until you find one that meets your needs. Then prepare a style sheet, template or written specification for it.

Make sure that everyone on your team knows what it is, and how they need to conform to it.

| Usability | |
|---|---|
| Style | ✓ |
| Programming | |

## Incorporate text into page layouts

Use the template to lay out the draft text.

Before showing it to anyone, check the navigational controls and hyperlinks so that you are confident enough to show it to your experts and customer.

| Usability | ✓ |
|---|---|
| Style | ✓ |
| Programming | |

## Test prototype with customer and make edits

Work through the prototype with the customer and make sure that they are happy with what you have developed so far.

Take account of any reservations they have about language and screen designs, but remember that you will have probably designed materials with a different target group to your customer in mind. You can be more confident to resist pressures for change if you have done solid research about them before you start the design and feel sure that you know why you have done what you have.

| Usability | ✓ |
|---|---|
| Style | ✓ |
| Programming | |

# Stage 2 – First draft

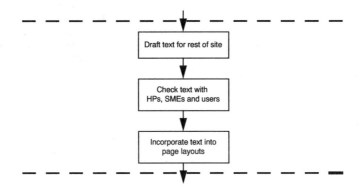

*Figure 9.3: First draft stage*

## Draft text for rest of site

Write out the rest of the content and prepare all the graphics you need.

Again, use colleagues and grammar checkers to weed out errors and ambiguities.

| | |
|---|---|
| Usability | ✓ |
| Style | |
| Programming | |

## Check text with HPs, SMEs and users

Go through the paper drafts with the high performers, subject matter experts and some users. It is important to test as much of the material as you can at this stage, as it gets much harder to edit text once it has been programmed into web pages.

| | |
|---|---|
| Usability | ✓ |
| Style | ✓ |
| Programming | |

If people find the content hard to understand when it is on paper, they will certainly find it hard when on screen. Do not worry too much at this stage about navigation from one section to another. Your proposed site navigation may make this part of the design clearer.

Here are some tips that can help to improve the effectiveness of your testing:

• Find users from as wide a cross-section of the user group as possible. You may well already have some volunteers if you planned this far ahead at the beginning of the project.

• Sit with people and watch them read through the text. Although this is time consuming, you will get much better feedback than if you send it to people and ask them to write comments on it.

- Tell the people it is not your work. People can sometimes feel reluctant to criticise another person's work to their face.

- Get users in groups of two to review the text. Pairs of people feel less intimidated than would one person about making criticisms, especially if they think it is your work. Two people will sit and talk to each other about it, and may forget you are there.

- Look carefully for their body language. Frowns, sitting back, 'hmms' can all be signs which show they do not understand what you have written.

## Incorporate text into page layouts

After making changes as a result of this stage of testing, paste the text into the page layouts. Add all the navigational controls and hyperlinks.

| Usability | ✓ |
| Style | ✓ |
| Programming | ✓ |

Test it thoroughly yourself. Ask colleagues to work through it as well. Use any software aids that you have: for example, FrontPage can check through a web for missing links.

# Stage 3 – Alpha testing

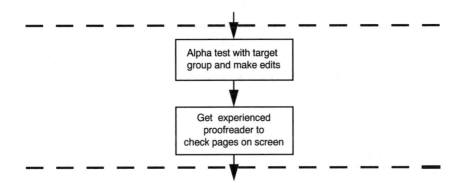

*Figure 9.4: Alpha testing*

## Alpha test with target group and make edits

There are two purposes of alpha testing:

| | |
|---|---|
| Usability | ✓ |
| Style | ✓ |
| Programming | ✓ |

- Finding mistakes in the basic content, such as typos and other misspellings that have slipped through the checks on the paper versions, and language problems that have not been noticed before. Text on screen can seem different to the same text on paper.

- Programming errors which mean that navigation and hyperlinks do not work.

The tips given in the previous stage on paper testing also apply here. In addition, look out for testers going back over previous pages – they may have lost the thread of the subject.

When you see or hear anything that looks like a comment on the material, make a note of the page URL and, if appropriate, ask them what they are looking at.

Repeat this with as many people as you have time for. Then work through all the comments you have gathered and make the necessary changes.

## Get experienced proofreader to check pages on screen

| | |
|---|---|
| Usability | ✓ |
| Style | ✓ |
| Programming | |

By the time you and your colleagues have read through the material two or three times, you will know it so well that you start subconsciously to skip pieces of text. That makes it very hard to spot the last few mistakes.

An external proofreader will be fresh to the subject, and should have been specially trained in techniques that will help them to spot the last little mistake.

Try to find someone who is familiar with reading through web-based material, so that they understand the two-dimensional nature of the content. If possible, give them the picture of the layout of the site that you copied down from your pin board exercise.

# Stage 4 – Beta testing

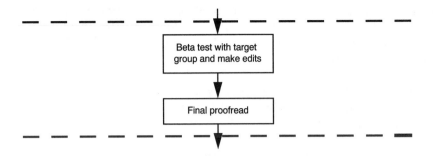

Figure 9.5: Beta testing

The purpose of beta testing is to see how well your materials work in real life. You may also pick up text and programming errors, but these should be minimal by this stage.

Beta testing will take place over a longer timescale and needs more organisation than alpha testing.

## Beta test with target group and make edits

| Usability | ✓ |
|---|---|
| Style | ✓ |
| Programming | ✓ |

First, find your beta test panel. Try to find a group of people that represents a cross-section of users, those with different levels of experience, from different departments, in different geographical locations and, if appropriate, those using different operating systems and browsers.

Gather them all together. Give a brief explanation of what you want them to do, but do not demonstrate the site. You want them to give it as real a test as possible. In real life you will not be able to give everyone in the organisation a demonstration of the material before they start using it. Agree when the test period will end. A week may be appropriate, but it depends on the scale of what you are asking them to do.

Testers will find their job easier if you can give them something in which to record their findings. A beta test log can simply contain pages with spaces for the person to write in the name or URL of a page and comments on that page. There is a blank table of this kind at the end of this section that you can photocopy and use if you wish.

The log should also ask the user to record what browser and operating system they are using, as this can make a difference to how pages display.

How to Design and Post Information on a Corporate Intranet

Explain to the test panel how they should use the test log. Decide whether you will collect their results daily, weekly or at the end of the test period.

Agree a date for everyone to get back together to discuss how they got on. For that meeting, it might be useful to find a neutral person to facilitate the discussion. People can feel reluctant to give negative feedback to someone they know designed something. That meeting should explore:

- what people liked about the materials

- what they did not like

- whether they found them useful

- what could be done to make them better

If you have not already done so, you should then collect in the test logs and start to analyse their comments. Look at:

- specific URLs – are there particular pages that give cause for comment?

- specific browsers and operating systems – do problems occur on a UNIX system but not on a PC, for example?

- whether there are particular areas in the material that could be improved

- how happy the users are with the look, feel and tone

- how easily they were able to find their way around

- how useful they found the information

## Final proofread

Once you have been through all the test logs and have implemented all the ideas that have come out the beta testing, you can now arrange to have the material finally proofread.

| Usability | ✓ |
|---|---|
| Style | ✓ |
| Programming | |

| URL | Comment |
|-----|---------|
|     |         |
|     |         |
|     |         |
|     |         |
|     |         |
|     |         |
|     |         |
|     |         |
|     |         |
|     |         |
|     |         |
|     |         |
|     |         |
|     |         |
|     |         |
|     |         |
|     |         |
|     |         |
|     |         |
|     |         |
|     |         |

How to Design and Post Information on a Corporate Intranet

## Stage 5 – Customer sign off

Figure 9.6: Customer sign off

### Customer signs off site

The last stage is to make sure that your customer is happy with it. If you have shown them the prototype and have kept them informed about your progress, you should be confident that they will sign it off without significant changes being needed.

| Usability | ✓ |
| Style | ✓ |
| Programming | ✓ |

Keep your fingers crossed that you have found and corrected all the programming errors. A dead hyperlink would be very embarrassing at this stage!

Following this quality management process should minimise the pain that can go with web development projects. It may seem that it will take more time doing it this way, but it will almost certainly save time and money in the end: not to mention a lot of your nervous energy.

With that done, you will now be able to release the site for general use. You may have to liaise with the team in overall charge of the intranet to arrange publicity for your new pages. This might be through an entry in a What's New section on the intranet home page, a mass e-mailing, an item in the in-house magazine (paper or electronic), or whatever seems appropriate.

You can then draw breath and think about the next project. But not for ever! Intranet materials lose a lot of their value if they are allowed to stagnate, and one of the advantages of the medium is that is easy to gather feedback and update materials. That is what the last chapter considers.

# Key points from the chapter

- You can only achieve quality by building it into the design and development process, not by adding it on at the end.

- You quality process must make sure that the site is useful, looks good and works technically.

# Chapter 10

# How to check the success of your site

# Chapter 10
## How to check the success of your site

After reading this chapter you will be able to:

> • set up a way of seeing how many people are using your site
>
> • describe what people think of the site
>
> • judge how effective your materials have been

If you have worked your way through the process described in this book, and have finally implemented your site, you can sit down and reflect on what a thorough job you have done.

This process will have made sure that, as far as you have been able, the site will meet the needs of the target group. However, you cannot be too complacent. Your testing process has involved a small, possibly statistically insignificant, number of people from the target group, and so you cannot be absolutely sure that you will have explained everything to everyone's satisfaction. Also things change as time goes by, and the issues covered by your site may change between the time you test it and implement it.

Unlike print, an intranet site can be changed almost instantaneously. If you realise that one paragraph is ambiguous, you can change it immediately: you do not have to arrange reprints or new editions or distribute erratum slips. Use this facility as much as you need. Do not see making changes as a sign of having 'got something wrong'.

Therefore, while you will now have time to make a cup of tea, your job is not yet finished. You need to develop ways of making sure that your site remains accurate, usable and popular.

We will look at a four-level way of doing this. This is based on work done by Donald Kirkpatrick into ways of evaluating training. He identified these four levels at which you can see how successful training (or in this context, information provision) has been:

| 1. Reaction | What were users' responses to the site? Did they like it? Did they think it looked attractive and well presented? Was it written at the right level for them? |
|---|---|
| 2. Learning | Did the users learn anything from the site? Were they able to do anything differently afterwards? |
| 3. Behaviour | After using the site, did users start doing their jobs differently? Did people continue to use the information? |
| 4. Results | Has the site been successful in raising users' performance in the way intended? |

We shall look at each level in turn and see how we can plan to gather appropriate information. This may not be easy. Some of these areas are very hard to research and it can be almost impossible to decide whether your site (or any other initiative) on its own has had any specific effect on raising performance.

The main emphasis in this chapter is on evaluation that you can directly relate to the site, which is essentially at Levels 1 and 2. It does look briefly at the other levels, but to do these properly is complex and calls for experience and skills in interviewing and statistical analysis.

# Level 1 – What are the users' reactions?

There are two things you can do here. You can add a counter to the site, so that you can see how many people use it, and you can provide users with a form with which they can give you feedback.

## Are people using the site?

It is possible to add special programming to your pages that will keep a record of each time a page is accessed. You may have seen such counters on pages on the Internet. How easy it is to do this depends on the HTML editor you are using, but your intranet support team will be able to help you with this.

The value of this is that you can get an idea of how useful the pages are. If only a handful of people have used the materials after two weeks, you will need to think about why this is.

## What do people think about your materials?

To keep your materials alive and up to date, you need to set up ways in which users can give you feedback. The simplest way to do this is by adding your telephone number or e-mail address to each page.

A more sophisticated way, and one that makes it even easier for users, is to design a form that you put somewhere within the material, perhaps on the home page. These forms allow a user to type in their comments, click a button and automatically send them to you. HTML has commands to enable you to create a form, but it does not help you to do anything with whatever the user types in. To process this information you need to write special programs that will manipulate this data.

These programs have to comply with what is called the *Common Gateway Interface*, or CGI. This is a software standard that defines how data entered on an HTML page will be processed. CGI programs (or scripts) can be written in a number of conventional programming languages, such as C, C++ or Perl, but this is a complex area that we cannot enter into here. If you need a CGI script, you will have to learn the necessary programming skills or find someone to do it for you.

What we want here is a program that takes the information entered by the user and converts it into a database format. We could then use our favourite database application to open the file and see what users have said. FrontPage provides some help in doing this. It comes with a number of built-in CGI functions, one of which is a form handler. We can see below how we might be able to use this.

First, you need to think about some issues regarding form design. How do you react to a form? With reluctance probably. Your users will as well, so if you want to have a form that users will actually take time to fill in, follow these guidelines.

| | |
|---|---|
| **Be clear about the purpose** | Decide what you want to find out, and design the form to do just that. Avoid adding in extra questions because you think they might be interesting. Do not forget that each extra question probably reduces the number of responses. |
| **Make it worthwhile to the user** | People will be more likely to fill in the form if they think it will benefit them in some way. This is why you often see 'This will help us to give you a better service' at the top of customer service questionnaires. So think about your purpose for the form and why filling it in will help the user. Will the information on the site be, for example, more useful, up to date or concise? |
| **Ask for easy information first** | Ask for straight factual information first, such as name, grade, etc. (if personal details are important, and they may well not be if you are looking for feedback at this level). Other factual information may be how many times they have used the site or how often they use the information each day. Move on to questions asking about their impressions of the site. |
| **Keep questions simple and unambiguous** | Make all questions one sentence long. Avoid questions that can mean anything, for example 'How well designed was the site?' could mean the structure, the page design or any number of other things. Do not ask two questions at the same time. Do not ask leading questions, such as: 'How attractive are the page layouts?' |
| **Test it out before going live** | If a question can be misunderstood, it will be. No matter how clear you think your questions are, there will be people who do not understand what they mean. So follow the quality process we looked at in Chapter 9:<br><br>1. Ask colleagues to read the questions first.<br><br>2. Test them with users on paper.<br><br>3. Test them with users on screen on a private web site.<br><br>4. Implement the form when you have removed every ambiguity you can find.<br><br>5. Review the answers you get and see whether they suggest any problems with the questions. |

We shall look at how you might do this for a project. This example would apply to any of the case studies we have looked at.

| | |
|---|---|
| **What is the purpose?** | We want to find out about users' reactions to the three main areas, usefulness, style and programming. Therefore we will ask one question about each of these. |
| **Make it worthwhile to the user** | Think about what reason would make someone think it useful to complete the form. This may be to keep the site accurate and reliable, or it could be so that their name is entered in a prize draw! |
| | Try this: |
| | ```
Please take a few minutes to answer the
questions below.  This will help us keep the
site up to date and as useful as possible.
``` |
| **Ask for easy information first** | In this case we are not going to ask for personal details, so the first question is as non-threatening as possible: |
| | ```
Is this the first time you have used this
site?
``` |
| **Keep questions simple and unambiguous** | We shall use two different types of question. For the questions on usefulness and style we shall use four-point Likert scales. These are questions where you ask the user to tick the box that they most agree with. Our questions will be: |
| | ```
Which of the following describes your
thoughts about the site:
Extremely useful
Fairly useful
Not very useful
Of no use to me

What are your thoughts about the look of the
site?
Very attractive
Fairly attractive
Looks quite ordinary
Not attractive
``` |
| | For the programming question, we shall ask a yes/no type question, and give the user space to type in details about any problems they found. |
| | ```
Did you find any hyperlinks that did not
work?
Yes  No

If you answered yes to the last question,
could you describe where you found the
problems?
``` |
| | These questions are worded simply, and the use of the Likert scale allows us to be clear about how we want the user to assess the site. |

Now that we have worked out the text, we can use FrontPage to put it together.

1. Open the FrontPage Editor, select File, New, Form Page Wizard, OK.

2. Click Next and type in a file name for the form page and its title. Click Next.

3. Click Add and you will see a list of question types. You can see what each one means by highlighting it. We want 'one of several options'.

4. Click in the edit box and type the question. It should look like this:

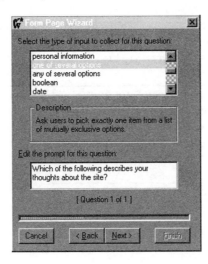

*Figure 10.1: Entering your question into the Form Page Wizard*

1. Click Next, and add the four labels. We will give the user radio buttons for them to click in, and shall name a variable that a database may need:

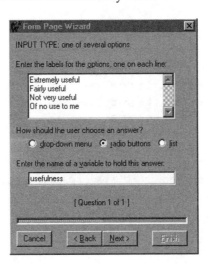

*Figure 10.2: Entering the question responses into the Form Page Wizard*

1. Click Next and repeat this for each question. For the yes/no question you choose 'boolean' and for entering information on programming problems choose 'paragraph'.

When you have typed in the last question click Next. Choose how you want to display the questions. Click Next.

How to Design and Post Information on a Corporate Intranet

Decide how you want to save the results. If you are going to collect the results to review later, choose to save the results to a text file. Click this button and enter the name of the file.

2. Click Next and you have finished.

You now return to the FrontPage Editor and see what you have created:

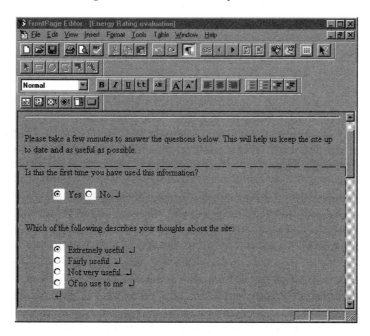

*Figure 10.3: The completed form in FrontPage Editor*

It will look very dull and mechanical. Don't worry, you can edit any of the text and can change the layout around to fit the style to the rest of the site. You can incorporate it into an existing page if you wish.

How to Design and Post Information on a Corporate Intranet

# Bibliography

The books listed below may help you if you are looking for more information on specific topics.

## Intranets in general:

Ryan Bernard, *The Corporate Intranet*, Wiley, New York, 1996

Shel Holtz, *The Intranet Advantage*, ZD Press, Emeryville, 1996

The Netscape World Wide Web site at http://home.netscape.com has various white papers about latest developments in the area.  Search through the site for current information.

## Microsoft FrontPage:

Neil Randall and Dennis Jones, *Using Microsoft Front Page*, Que, Indianapolis, 1996

## Page design:

There are a large number of books available on this subject, and you will probably want to choose one that suits your own needs and taste.  However, there are a large number of sites on the World Wide Web that you can read for free.

Mary Morris and Randy Hinrichs, *Web Page Design*, Prentice Hall, Upper Saddle River, 1996

*The Yale Style Manual* at http://info.med.yale.edu/caim

Sun Microcomputers' guide at http://www.sun.com/styleguide/

David Siegel's site at http://www.killersites.com (which complements his book on the subject)

For current information, use Yahoo and its categorised listing.

## Clear writing:

Martin Cutts, *The Plain English Guide*, Oxford University Press, Oxford, 1996

## Designing interactive training materials:

Nigel Harrison, *Practical Instructional Design for Open Learning Materials*, McGraw-Hill, Maidenhead, 1995

How to Design and Post Information on a Corporate Intranet

# Develop your knowledge and skills further

ACT Consultants run a number of intranet workshops and seminars based on the principles outlined in this book.

This is your chance to practise your skills, develop your knowledge and learn from the experts.

**Call for details**

0114 278 0798

**or write to us at:**

ACT Consultants Ltd
Arundel Street
Sheffield Science Park
Sheffield
S1 2NS

Network with the author:

I would love to have your feedback on the ideas I've presented in this book or perhaps meet you on a workshop.

**Send me an e-mail at:**

act@fdgroup.co.uk

Bryan Hopkins